MY BEST
SELF-WORKING
CARD TRICKS

Karl Fulves

With 116 Illustrations by
Joseph K. Schmidt

DOVER PUBLICATIONS, INC.
Mineola, New York

Bibliographical Note

My Best Self-Working Card Tricks is a new work, first published by
Dover Publications, Inc., in 2001.

Library of Congress Cataloging-in-Publication Data

Fulves, Karl.
    My best self-working card tricks / Karl Fulves ; with 116 illustrations
by Joseph K. Schmidt.
        p. cm.
    ISBN-13: 0-486-41981-7 (pbk.)
    ISBN-10: 0-486-41981-9 (pbk.)
    1. Card tricks. I. Title.
GV1549 .F85 2001
793.8'5—dc21

                                                                2001042345

Manufactured in the United States by LSC Communications
41981906   2017
www.doverpublications.com

INTRODUCTION

Self-working card tricks are an important part of the magician's bag
of tricks. Even if a magician can perform card manipulation by
means of advanced sleight of hand, he will incorporate self-working
tricks into his performance. There are a number of reasons for this.
Perhaps most important is the fact that if a magician relies solely on
sleight of hand, spectators will soon catch on that secret manipulation is at work. If the magician weaves self-working tricks into his
performance, the audience is not sure what to think. Another reason
is that on occasion a magician will be asked to perform in impromptu circumstances with borrowed cards. If the cards are worn,
they are not easily manipulated. Under these conditions, the magician can fall back on self-working card tricks that do not require
manipulation.

Magic is a performance art. Practice each trick so its working is
second nature. Then perform before friends and family. Appraise the
strength of each effect. Many magicians, even working profession-
als, constantly reevaluate their tricks and do not hesitate to make
changes that strengthen audience impact. If a trick doesn't get the
desired reaction, consider ways to make the trick stronger.
Sometimes it's only a matter of finding just the right presentation or
patter story.

Although the title of this book is *My Best Self-Working Card Tricks*,
it is perhaps just a bit more precise to say that these are some of the
best such tricks I perform. The idea for this book was suggested by
the founder of Dover Publications, Hayward Cirker, and it is to him
that this book is dedicated. I would also like to thank Joseph K.
Schmidt for suggestions that strengthen this collection, and for art-
work that illuminates the text.

KARL FULVES

CONTENTS

PERSONALITY TESTS

People like to gain insight into their own lives, and will spend time and money consulting astrologers, fortune-tellers and tarot card readers. The tricks in this chapter make playing cards appear to tell people things about themselves.

1. Someone Like You

Some of the more memorable tricks are those that deal on a personal level with a spectator. In this trick you will need three slips of paper. They have writing on one side, but the writing is not shown right away. On the other side are the words shown in Figure 1. The spectator shuffles some cards and picks five. They are sorted according to color. If there are five of one color, he picks the leftmost piece of paper in Figure 1. If there are four of one color and one of the opposite color (for example, four reds and one black), he picks the middle piece of paper. If there are three of one color and two of the opposite color, he picks the rightmost piece of paper.

Fig. 1

When he has chosen a slip of paper, the other pieces are turned over. They describe personality types, but clearly they do not match the spectator's personality. When the chosen paper is turned over, the wording on the other side *exactly* describes the spectator's personality.

Method: You must know something about the spectator before you perform the trick. The spectator can be a friend, a relative or a friend of a friend. On a piece of paper jot down the spectator's traits, his hobbies, his job, and so forth. Turn this paper over and on the blank side write, "THREE AND TWO." On the other slips of paper jot down characteristics that are far different from the spectator's. Turn both of them over. On the blank side of one write, "FIVE ALIKE." On the blank side of the other write, "FOUR AND ONE." This is the only preparation.

Any deck may be used. Hold the cards so you can see the faces. Remove a pair of cards consisting of a black card on top, a red card below it, and place this pair face down on the table. Find three more pairs with a black on top, a red on the bottom, and place each onto the tabled cards. The eight-card packet will be stacked black-red-black-red-black-red-black-red from top to bottom.

Now find a pair consisting of a red card on top, a black card below it, and place this pair face down on the table. Find three more pairs with a red on top, a black on the bottom, and place each pair onto the tabled pair. The eight-card packet will be stacked red-black-red-black and so on from top to bottom.

Fig. 2

Ask the spectator to riffle shuffle the two groups of cards together, Figure 2. He performs the riffle shuffle just once. Then have him deal the top five cards to himself. Because he shuffled the two groups of cards randomly together, it would seem that the top five cards are a truly random distribution of colors. But there will always be three of one color and two of the other.

The piece of paper that matches this outcome is the one on the right in Figure 1. Turn the other slips of paper over and read aloud the descriptions. Clearly, they do not describe him. Turn over the remaining piece and read the character description. It exactly describes the spectator's personality.

2. The Odd Couple

The magician remarks, "We all have had the experience of meeting a happily married couple and wondering how two such opposite types get along so well. In the world of playing cards, odd couples are represented by the odd cards." The magician deals the odd hearts in a layout like the one shown in Figure 3. "The ace of hearts is going to marry one of the prospective suitors represented by the three, five, seven and nine."

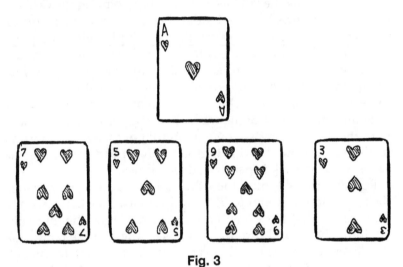

Fig. 3

The ♥3, ♥5, ♥7 and ♥9 are gathered and shuffled by the spectator. While the magician turns his back, the spectator selects one of these four cards as the card she thinks will be most congenial with the ♥A. The magician does not know which card was selected. Let's say it is the ♥3.

The ♥3, ♥5, ♥7 and ♥9 are then shuffled back into the deck. The spectator may shuffle and cut the cards. The magician takes back the deck. "Let's see if you guessed who the ace of hearts chose." The magician removes one card from the deck. It is the ♥3, the very card selected by the spectator.

Method: The secret is given in Figure 3, but it is well concealed and almost impossible to decipher unless one knows what to

Fig. 4

look for. In a deck of cards, there are certain cards which magicians refer to as pointer cards or one-way cards. The odd-value hearts are examples of such cards. Looking at the ♥3, Figure 4, the center heart pip has one pointed end which can point up or down. In Figure 4, it points up.

Look again at Figure 3, and you will see that the center pip of each of the four cards below the ♥A has its center pip pointing upwards. If one of those cards is turned around end-for-end, the magician will know which it is because the center pip will now point downwards. This is the basis for the trick. (It does not matter which way the ♥A points, since this card does not figure into the method.) It is best to orient the four odd-value hearts the same way before the trick begins to avoid a lot of suspicious twisting and turning of the cards. You can perform other tricks with the deck as long as you are careful not to turn any portion of the deck around. With the odd-value hearts pointing the same way, the trick is performed as follows.

Remove the ♥A plus the other odd-value hearts. Arrange them as shown in Figure 3, as you remark that these are the four suitors that the ♥A will choose from. Gather the four suitors into a heap, and turn the heap face down on the table. Ask the spectator to cut the four-card heap and complete the cut, then to give it another complete cut. Point out that this randomizes the positions of the four suitors. Now cut the deck into two heaps and say, "The ace of hearts chose one of these suitors to be her companion. I'd like you to guess which one." As you tap the packet on the right say, "Deal three of the cards onto this heap. This represents the rejected suitors." After the spectator has done this, have her deal the remaining card onto the packet on the left. This represents the suitor chosen by the spectator.

Lift off the card on the left-hand packet. Tilt it up so the spectator can see the face of the card. "I'd like you to remember the identity of the suitor you chose. We'll see if this matches the one chosen by the ace of hearts." Return the card to the top of

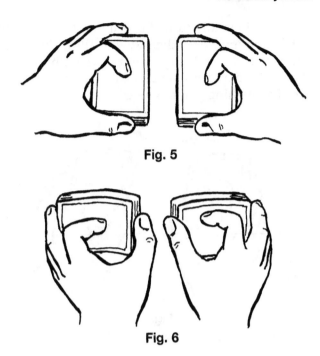

Fig. 5

Fig. 6

the left-hand packet, and ask her to cut each packet and complete the cut. After she has given each packet a cut, grasp the
packets as shown in Figure 5. You are going to shuffle them by
a procedure invented by Theodore Annemann.

Turn the packets toward one another, Figure 6. This is a subtle way of reversing the packets end-for-end. Riffle shuffle the
two halves of the deck together and square up the deck. Ask
the spectator to give the deck an additional shuffle and cut.
Spread the cards so you can see the faces. Look at the faces of
the ♥3, ♥5, ♥7 and ♥9, specifically at the center pip. One of
these four cards will have the center pip facing in the opposite
direction from the pips in the other cards. This is the card chosen by the spectator. Remove this card from the deck and say,
"Here's the card chosen by the ace of hearts. Which card did
you nominate for that honor?" The spectator names the card
she chose. Turn over the card in hand to reveal she chose the
correct suitor.

In tricks using one-way or pointer cards, it is important that no cards are accidentally turned end-for-end. In this trick, that possibility is minimized by the way you allow the spectator to handle the cards. Since the spectator does nothing more than deal three cards to one heap and one to the other heap, there is little risk of something going wrong.

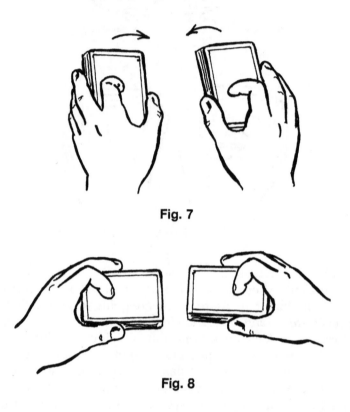

Fig. 7

Fig. 8

Many people riffle shuffle cards by the method shown in Figures 5 and 6. Magicians use a different method called the end riffle. It produces the same result but it looks more professional. Grasp the cards by the sides, near the inner ends, as shown in Figure 7. Turn the packets toward one another in the direction of the arrows in Figure 7. The packets are now in the position shown in Figure 8. Shuffle them together, square up the deck and give it a cut. The spectator can also give the deck a shuffle, but make sure that no cards are accidentally turned end-for-end.

3. Compatibility

In this trick, the magician demonstrates how the science of numerology reveals whether or not two people are compatible with one another. The trick should be done for a husband and wife, or a boyfriend and girlfriend.

The lady mixes a deck of cards, turns the deck face up and removes any eight cards, then seven more, then six more, and then five more. She gives the balance of the deck to her boyfriend or husband. She gathers her cards into a common heap and holds the packet face up in her hand. Her boyfriend holds the remainder of the deck face down in his hand. The lady slowly deals her cards one at a time into two heaps, red cards in one heap, blacks in another. Her two heaps are shown as A and B in Figure 9.

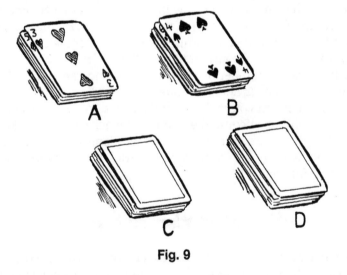

Fig. 9

The gentleman simultaneously deals cards off the top of his face-down packet into two heaps, C and D, but he does not look at the faces of his cards. He matches the way the lady deals. In other words, if the first two cards in her heap are red, she would deal these two cards into heap A. The gentleman deals the top two cards of his packet sight unseen into heap C. If the next three cards in the lady's packet are black, she would deal these three cards face up into heap B. The gentleman deals the top three cards of his heap face down into heap D.

At the finish, there will be two face-up heaps (A and B) in front of the lady. Heap A will contain only red cards. Heap B will contain only black cards. There will be two face-down heaps in front of the gentleman, C and D. Each of his heaps will contain a random mixture of reds and blacks. Point to the face-up cards in front of the lady and say, "These cards reflect attributes we can all see in someone. The number of reds in the first heap and the number of blacks in the second heap indicate that one partner is tall, the other short. One is quiet, the other outgoing." (Simply describe the two people engaged in the test.)

Now tap the face-down heaps. "These represent qualities that are hidden—personality, character, spirit, soul. We're going to focus on the red cards over here [tap packet C] and the black cards over here [tap packet D]. If there are far more reds in one heap than there are blacks in the other, it means that two people are incompatible. The closer the numbers are to one another, the better the two people match up. On very rare occasions, one in a million, the two people are so well matched that there are exactly the same number of reds over here [indicate packet C] as there are blacks over here [indicate packet D]."

Ask the lady to count the number of red cards in packet C. Have the gentleman count the number of black cards in packet D. They will always be equal to one another. Congratulate the lucky couple on being one in a million. The trick works every time if you use a full deck of fifty-two cards.

4. Most Wanted List

The magician remarks, "Computers can now be equipped with a program called Astro Logic. The program analyzes your personality so it can help you find your perfect mate. Science tells us there are personality types. Some of the most typical are listed here in what is called—for some reason—a Most Wanted List." The list is shown in Figure 10. Read off the first four or five lines, and place the list face down on the table.

The spectator is asked to think of two of the digits in her date of birth. If her birthdate is June 27, 1985, the digits would be

6-2-7-1-9-8-5. Ask her to think of two of the digits. We will assume she picks 5 and 7, although she tells no one of her choices.

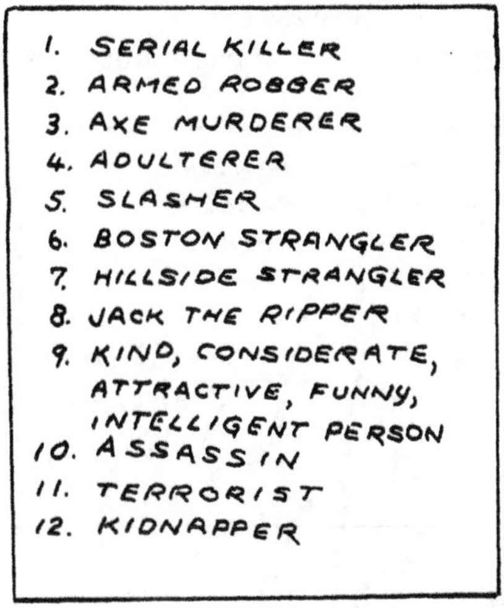

Before the trick started you placed any 9-spot on top of the deck. Holding the deck in your left hand, ask her to tell you the larger of the two digits. In our example she would say 7. Push off a packet of seven cards without reversing their order. Place this packet

```
1.  SERIAL KILLER
2.  ARMED ROBBER
3.  AXE MURDERER
4.  ADULTERER
5.  SLASHER
6.  BOSTON STRANGLER
7.  HILLSIDE STRANGLER
8.  JACK THE RIPPER
9.  KIND, CONSIDERATE,
    ATTRACTIVE, FUNNY,
    INTELLIGENT PERSON
10. ASSASSIN
11. TERRORIST
12. KIDNAPPER
```

Fig. 10

on the table. The top card of the packet is the 9-spot. Turn your head to one side, and ask her to focus now on the smaller of the two digits. She is to silently count that many cards onto the tabled heap. In our example, she would count five cards onto the heap of seven cards. She does not tell you how many cards she dealt.

Turn and face the audience. Square the packet. "You have entered two digits into the Astro Logic program. We know only one of those numbers, the seven, so we will use it twice." Deal seven cards, one at a time, from the top of the packet to the table. Drop the balance of the packet on top. Again deal seven cards to the table, but stop when you have dealt the seventh card. Push this card in front of the lady and say, "One number is known, one unknown, symbolizing in turn controlled and random elements in our lives. Turn over that card. See what the number is and then consult that number on the chart. We will know soon enough if Astro Logic has correctly analyzed you." The lady turns over the playing card. It shows the number 9. Consulting the ninth entry on the Most Wanted List, she can't deny that the description fits her to a "T."

All the start of the trick when the lady hears that the possible personality types include serial killer, armed robber, axe murderer and so on, she will expect the worst. Present the trick in a

lighthearted way, making it all seem a bit of a joke. When showing the list at the beginning, obscure the one positive entry at

position 9 by keeping the hand over the list, Figure 11.

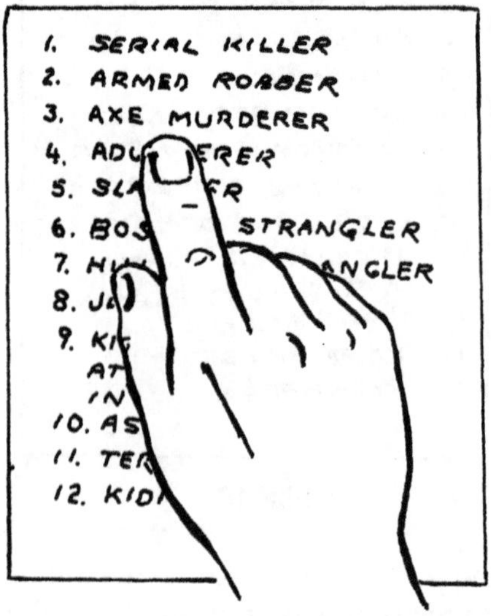

1. SERIAL KILLER
2. ARMED ROBBER
3. AXE MURDERER
4. ADULTERER
5. SLAYER
6. BOSTON STRANGLER
7. HILLSIDE STRANGLER
8. JA
9. KI
   AT
   IN
10. AS
11. TER
12. KID

Fig. 11

After you have read off the first five or six character types, turn the list over and keep it near- er to you than to her to discourage anyone from turning it over to read the rest of the list. At the end of the trick, she will be surprised to learn that Astro Logic got her per- sonality exactly right.

This trick is based on a principle invented by Stewart James.

IMPROMPTU TRICKS

People sometimes suspect magicians of using trick decks. They will even voice doubt that magicians can perform card magic with ordinary playing cards. For this reason, it is important to have on hand a repertoire of tricks that can be performed with any deck that is handed to you. The tricks in this chapter use borrowed cards and can be performed on the spot.

5. Calculated Cut

In many cards tricks, the magician must have secret information about the deck, or he must perform secret manipulation at some point in the trick. This trick is an exception. The magician has no information and has nothing to do but perform the actions described here. If the instructions are followed correctly, he will locate two freely chosen cards under strict conditions. The trick gets its name from the fact that it originally used a sleight-of-hand method of cutting the cards to get the desired outcome. In this version, all sleights have been eliminated.

Method: The deck must contain fifty-two cards. Turn your head to one side and ask someone to shuffle the cards. He is to then remove a small number of cards from the top of the deck, any quantity between one and ten cards. He counts these cards and hides them in his pocket. Whatever number of cards he takes, he is to remember the card that lies at the same number from the top of the deck. For example, if he pocketed eight cards, he would remember the card that now lies eighth from the top of the deck.

Turn and face the spectator and say, "I'm going to have another card chosen, but I don't want someone to choose the same card this gentleman chose. That would be too easy." As you speak, take the deck in your left hand. Push off exactly sixteen cards without reversing their order and place them off to one side on the table. Hand the remainder of the deck to a lady. "Please shuffle these cards. Lift off a group of cards. The number is not important. Look at the face card of the group you cut off, and then place that packet on top of these cards." Tap the sixteen-card packet. The lady places her cards on top of the sixteen-card packet.

Say, "You still have some cards left over. I want this to be as difficult as possible for me—no tricks, no cheating—so please shuffle the remaining cards and place them on top of all." When the spectator has done this, square the deck and place it face down in the left hand. You do not know the identity of either card. You don't even know how many cards are in the deck. Yet, without asking a question, you are going to locate each of the chosen cards. It is done as follows.

Ask the first spectator to get a clear mental picture of his card. Begin dealing cards off the top of the deck into a face-up heap on the table. Pause every now and then as if studying a particular card. It seems as if you are looking for clues, but what you are really doing is silently counting the cards as you deal them. Deal thirty-five cards off the top into the face-up heap. When you get to the thirty-sixth card, stop. Don't turn this card face up.

Look at the first spectator and say, "What card did you choose?" He might name the ♣9. Turn up the card in hand. It will be the ♣9. Toss this card to the table in front of the first spectator and say to him, "We still have to find the lady's card. I'm going to ask your help on this. You have some cards in your pocket. I'm going to put these cards in my pocket."

Pick up the thirty-five-card packet and place it in your pocket. Instruct the first spectator to remove cards from his pocket one at a time. As he does this, you match him card for card, but remove cards from the face or bottom of your packet. The process continues until he has dealt his last card. In our example, he would remove eight cards from his pocket. You would match him card for card. When you have your eighth card in hand, he announces that he has no more cards in his pocket. Turn over the card you are holding and it will be the card chosen by the second spectator.

Some of the tricks in this book make use of pencil-dotted cards. If you are using your own deck to perform "Calculated Cut," a pencil-dotted card can be used to shortcut some of the counting. After doing other tricks, arrange to have the pencil-dotted card sixteenth from the top of the deck. Place the deck face up on the table. Ask a spectator to cut off any number of cards from one to ten. He is to count the cards and hide them in his pocket. After he has done this, spread the face-up deck across the table. Ask him to remember the card that is the same number from the top as the number of cards in his pocket. When he has a card in mind, gather the deck and turn it face down. Quickly spread the cards from hand to hand until you spot the pencil-dotted card. This card is still sixteenth from the top, so it is an easy matter to cut off the top sixteen cards and place this packet on the table. The trick now proceeds with the selection of the second card and the double revelation as already described.

As to why the trick works, a classic principle is in operation. Remove a packet of cards from a fifty-two-card deck. The packet can contain from one to ten cards. Count the number of cards in the packet. Look at and remember the card that lies at the same number from the top of the deck. If, for instance, you removed ten cards, you would look at the card that now lies tenth from the top. Push sixteen cards off the top of the deck without reversing their order. Transfer this packet to the bottom of the deck. The chosen card is now thirty-sixth from the top.

6. Sherlock's Card

"The magician detective John Sherlock Jr. invented an unusual way of finding a chosen card. Let's see if Junior's trick will work with this deck of cards." The spectator gives the magician a small group of cards from the deck. The magician picks one of these, say the ♥4, writes the detective's name on it, turns the ♥4 face up and inserts it into the packet.

From the rest of the deck the spectator takes a portion of cards, shuffles them and notes the face card, say the ♦J. The deck is assembled. The detective card is located. The writing on it says "JOHN JR." The spectator spells J-O-H-N J-R, dealing a card for each letter. When the last dealt card is turned up, it is indeed the chosen card, the ♦J. Any deck may be used.

Method: Some tricks are designed so that the method is shaped by external factors. In this trick, the name you write on the detective card depends on the number of cards in the packet.

Ask the spectator to shuffle the deck and hand you a small group of cards. Almost always he will hand you fewer than fifteen cards. If not, ask him to give you a smaller number. Remark that you want to look through the cards to find the all-important detective card. This is what you say, but what you do is to silently count the cards in the packet. If the packet contains an even number of cards, use that number. If the packet contains an odd number of cards, silently advance to the next number. For example, if the packet contains nine cards, use the number ten.

Remove any card from the packet and place it on the face of the packet. The name you write depends on the number you are keeping in mind. The system is shown in Figure 12. If you counted six cards in the packet, you would write the name "JOHN JR." on the card. If you counted seven cards, keeping in mind that seven is an odd number, silently advance to the next number to arrive at eight. Looking at the chart in Figure 12, you know that the name you will write on the card is "SHERLOCK."

(<u>SYSTEM</u>)

2	= J R
4	= JOHN
6	= JOHN JR
8	= SHERLOCK
10	= SHERLOCK JR
12	= JOHN SHERLOCK
14	= JOHN SHERLOCK JR

Fig. 12

Place the card and the packet behind the back. Remark that you will insert the card at a random location in the packet. Really, turn it face up and place it on the bottom of the packet. Bring the packet back into view and place it face down on the table. Ask the spectator to lift off a bunch of cards from the remainder of the deck, shuffle the packet and remember the face or bottom card. He then drops this packet on top of your packet. Pick up the combined packet and place it on top of the deck.

"We have to start with the detective card." Deal cards one at a time off the top of the deck into a heap on the table. Stop when you have dealt the face-up detective card onto the heap. Put the rest of the deck aside, and read the name you have written on the card. Then spell it out a letter at a time, starting with the face-up card, dealing a card off the packet for each letter. If the heap that was given to you at the beginning of the trick contained an even number of cards, turn up the new top card of the deck and it will be the chosen card. If the heap given to you at the beginning contained an odd number of cards, turn up the last dealt card and it will be the chosen card.

An example of each case would be as follows. The spectator gives you a packet of eight cards. From the chart of Figure 12, you will have written "SHERLOCK" on the face of the detective card. Proceed with the trick to the point where the deck has been assembled. You are ready to spell out the detective's name. Spell S-H-E-R-L-O-C-K, dealing a card for each letter. Turn up the top card of the deck and it will be the chosen card.

If, at the beginning, the spectator handed you a packet of seven cards, silently advance one to arrive at eight. Write "SHERLOCK" on the face of the detective card. Proceed with the trick up to the point where the deck has been assembled. Spell S-H-E-R-L-O-C-K, dealing a card for each letter. Turn up the last card dealt and it will be the chosen card.

7. Out on Location

The magician writes a number on one piece of paper, the name of a card on another. He folds the slips of paper and places them to one side. Each of two spectators chooses cards from the deck. The deck is assembled. One of the papers is opened, revealing that one of the chosen cards will be fifteenth from the top of the deck. The fifteenth card is counted to, and it is indeed the first chosen card. The deck is then spread face up on the table. The second spectator is invited to push his card out of the spread. This card may be the ♣5. The second paper is opened. It correctly predicts that the ♣5 would be chosen. Any deck of cards may be used for this trick. The deck need not be complete.

Method: This trick was worked out by Roy Walton and the author. When you get the deck, spread it face up between the hands. Tell the audience that you are looking for a good combination of numbers. Secretly note the card that lies fifteenth from the face of the deck. Say this card is the ♦K. Close up the deck and place it face down on the table. On a piece of paper write the number fifteen (it is always fifteen). On a separate piece of paper write "KING OF DIAMONDS." Fold each slip of paper and toss them onto the table.

Invite spectator A to remove a group of cards from the top of the deck, any number of cards from one to ten. Turn the deck face up. Invite spectator B to remove a similarly small number of cards from the face of the deck. Then ask spectator A to count his cards. Let's say he counts five cards. Deal cards off the face of the deck into a face-up heap. When you get to the fifth card, ask him to remember this card. Continue dealing until you have dealt fourteen cards. As you deal, say, "You could, of course, have chosen any one of these cards." Replace the fourteen-card packet on the face of the deck.

Now turn attention to spectator B. Ask him to count his cards. Say he has eight cards. Deal eight cards into a heap from the face of the deck, and ask him to remember the eighth card. Then continue dealing until you have dealt a total of fourteen cards. As you deal, say, "And, of course, it is also true in your case that you could have chosen any one of these cards." There is a fourteen-card packet face up on the table. You hold a face-up packet in your hand. Place your packet on top of the tabled packet. Take spectator B's cards and place them on the face of the deck. Turn the deck face down and hold it in the left hand. Then take spectator A's cards and place them on top of all. The deck has now been reassembled.

Have the first prediction slip opened and read aloud. It says that one of the cards will be fifteenth from the top of the deck. Count fifteen cards. Turn over the last card dealt and it will be spectator A's card. Now spread the deck face up on the table, and ask spectator B to slide his card out of the spread. Direct someone to open the other prediction slip. It correctly predicts the identity of spectator B's card.

8. Hidden Power

Jack Avis devised a streamlined version of a trick where a randomly chosen card at an unknown location in the deck ends up at a location freely designated by another spectator. I've added a twist to this fine trick. The deck may be borrowed, with the only stipulation that it is a complete deck of fifty-two cards.

As you mix the cards, glimpse the bottom card of the deck. Say this card is the ♦2. Place the deck on the table. Turn your back. Ask spectator A to think of a number from one to ten. He is to deal two heaps of cards, each containing the chosen number. Caution him to deal silently so you don't know the chosen number. When he has done this, ask him to place one of the heaps in his pocket. He looks at the bottom card of the other heap and then drops this heap on top of the deck. Have someone place the deck in your hand, behind your back.

Say to the audience, "I don't know the card selected by this gentleman, nor do I know where it is in the deck. For that matter, I don't even know how many cards are in the deck at this point." Turning to a second party, spectator B, say, "I'd like you to help me. So that we don't duplicate the number chosen by this gentleman, please name any number between twenty and forty."

Assume that spectator B names thirty-seven. "I'm going to attempt to relocate the chosen card, moving it from an unknown location to a location that is exactly thirty-seven cards down from the top of the deck. This would be impossible unless I am able to pick up the thought waves of this gentleman." Turning to spectator A, say, "Sir, please concentrate on the card you chose."

Turn and face the audience. The cards are now out of sight behind your back. Whatever number chosen by spectator B, begin your count on the next number. In our example that would be thirty-eight. Silently push over cards one at a time from the top of the deck, counting thirty-eight, thirty-nine, forty, and so on up to and including fifty-two.

When you have done this, transfer this packet to the bottom of the deck. As surprising as it may seem, the chosen card is now exactly thirty-seven from the top of the deck. Bring the deck into view. Place it on the table in front of spectator B and say, "Sir, please count to the thirty-seventh card." The spectator does this, counting cards one at a time into a heap on the table. When the thirty-seventh card has been reached, turn to spectator A. "Please tell us the name of your card and its original position." The spectator might say that his original number was seven and his card was the ♠4. "Let's see if we have succeeded in moving the four of spades from position seven to position thirty-seven in the deck." Direct spectator B to turn over the thirty-seventh card. It will be the chosen card, the ♠4.

Now comes the twist that seems to prove that you did indeed know which number spectator A had chosen. Turn to spectator A and say, "Please remove the cards from your pocket. Count them so the audience can see that you did pick the number seven." When this has been done, direct attention to the packet just dealt by spectator B. In our example, he dealt a packet of thirty-seven cards and turned up the top card to show that it was the ♠4. Place the ♠4 aside, and say to the audience, "While this gentleman [spectator A] was thinking of a card and a number, I was too. Amazingly enough, my number was also seven, and my card was the two of diamonds." Direct spectator B to deal seven cards off the heap he just dealt. When he has done this, have him turn over the top card of this heap. It will be the ♦2.

The entire trick can be done with your head turned to one side so you don't see any cards from start to finish. Beforehand, remove one card from the deck. Let's say this card is the ♦2. Conceal it under your belt in back, or in a back trouser pocket. When ready to perform the trick, turn your head to one side so you can't see the cards. Ask spectator A to shuffle the deck and deal two equal heaps. He pockets one heap, looks at the face card of the other heap and drops this heap on top of the deck.

On a piece of paper write, "I'm thinking of the two of diamonds." The ♦2 is the card you secretly removed from the deck. Fold the paper and place it in plain view on the table. Take the deck behind your back, and then turn and face the audience. The cards are now out of sight behind your back. Quietly remove the ♦2 from its hiding place and place it on the bottom of the deck. From this point on, the trick proceeds exactly as written. Ask spectator B to name a number from twenty to forty. Starting on the next number, push over that many cards off the top of the deck, silently counting to fifty-two. Transfer that packet to the bottom of the deck.

Bring the deck into view. Spectator A names his card and his number. Have spectator B count off his chosen number of cards into a heap on the table. The last card will be A's chosen card. Spectator B now picks up the dealt packet and counts down to A's number. The last card of the count will be the ♦2. Turn this card face up. Then have the piece of paper unfolded and opened so the audience can see that you were on the same wavelength as spectator A.

9. Eleven and One

Transposition tricks usually require sleight of hand for their working. This trick, a transposition between four aces and four jacks, uses no sleights to achieve the desired end.

Spread the cards so you can see the faces. Upjog the four jacks, strip them out of the deck and place them face up on the table. Drop the face-up deck on top of them. Pick up the deck, and spread it between the hands again. Remove the aces as you come to them, tossing them to the table into a heap. Drop the deck on top of the aces. Pick up the deck, turn it face down and place it in the left hand. There are now four aces on top of the deck, with the four jacks beneath them.

The key maneuver comes into play at this point. Spread the top *seven* cards as you say, "Four aces and four jacks." Take this packet with the right hand. The left hand places the deck on the table. Place the packet into the left hand. The audience thinks you're holding eight cards in the left hand, but really you hold seven. You will proceed from this point to deal cards one at a time from the top to the bottom of the packet. When you come to the last jack (or what is perceived to be the last jack) on each round, you will place this card before the spectator.

Begin by transferring each of the four top cards to the bottom of the packet. As you do, say, "One, two, three, four aces." Pause, then continue the count, saying, "And one, two, three, four jacks. I'll give you the last jack." Hand the spectator what is apparently the fourth jack. Now the count is repeated. "One, two, three, four aces," as you transfer the top four cards one at a time from top to bottom. Then, "One, two, three jacks. You get the last jack again." Hand the last card of the jack count to the spectator. Again transfer cards one at a time from top to bottom, saying, "One, two, three, four aces, and one, two jacks. You get the last jack once more." Hand the last card of the jack count to the spectator.

"One final round. We have one, two, three, four aces and one jack." Transfer cards one at a time from top to bottom. When you get to the "one" jack, give this card to the spectator. Apparently the spectator has the four jacks. But unknown to the spectator, you are holding three (and not four) cards in your hand at this point. Place this packet on top of the deck to erase the one clue to the secret. Direct attention to the spectator's cards and say, "I'll pay you a dollar if you can tell me which of the cards you hold is the jack of spades." Whatever card he guesses, he turns that card face up, only to discover that it is not a jack but an ace. The other cards are turned up and prove to be the other three aces. All that remains is to deal the top four cards off the deck into a face-up row to complete the transposition between aces and jacks.

"Eleven and One" can be done as a poker trick. As the deal is done, remark that a gambler was given the four jacks in a poker game, a hand he knew to be inferior to the dealer's hand. After the spectator holds what he believes to be the four jacks say, "So the gambler switched cards on him." Turn up the top four cards of the deck to reveal the jacks. The spectator turns up his cards, showing that he now has the winning hand of four aces.

KLONDYKE SHUFFLE

When most people shuffle the deck, the intent is to randomly mix the cards. Magicians have the added option of mixing cards in such a way as to bring about a controlled result. The Klondyke shuffle is one such stratagem. It is said that the shuffle got its name from its use in card games during the Klondike gold rush in northern Canada, when the cold weather prevented numbed hands from shuffling cards by more conventional means. Others have speculated that it was used to mix cards in a solitaire game called Klondike. In any case, the Klondyke shuffle is a valuable tool in the magician's arsenal. Some of its uses are described in this chapter, while other tricks in this book also make use of it.

10. Turn Three Times

Simple methods sometimes create as much mystery as more complex secrets. The method to this trick is simple, but it is well concealed. The trick is basically a location of a chosen card, but a bit of window dressing has been added.

Ask the spectator to shuffle his own deck. He is then to turn the top half face up and place it on top of the bottom half. The two halves of the deck are now pointed in opposite directions, i.e., the top half is face up and the bottom half face down. Now, take the deck from the spectator. Secretly remember the identity of the face-up card you see on top of the deck. Let's say it is the ♦5. Turn your head to the right so it is clear that you are not looking at the cards and say, "In order for this trick to work, we are obliged to turn the deck over three times." Turn the deck over. Turn it over again. Then turn it over a third time. The ♦5 is no longer on top of the deck. Still keeping your gaze averted, grasp the deck from above with the right hand in preparation for the Klondyke shuffle. The right fingers are at the front short end of the deck and the thumb at the near short end. The grip is shown in Figure 13.

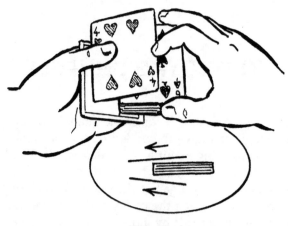

Fig. 13

"I'm going to deal cards off like this." Grasp the top card of the deck with the left thumb and the bottom card with the left fingers. Draw this pair of cards off the deck as shown in Figure 13. Place the pair on the table and say, "As I do this, please say 'stop' at any time." Continue drawing pairs of cards off the deck as in Figure 13. Place them into a heap on the table. When the spectator calls "stop," if you have a pair of cards in hand, drop them onto the tabled heap. Put the rest of the deck aside.

There will be a face-up card on top of the tabled heap. Say, "Please remember the top card. Then give the heap a cut." When the spectator has done this, say, "Give it another cut, and another." When the spectator has given the packet three cuts, turn and face him. Take the packet into the left hand and say, "I don't know why, but the trick only works if the cards are turned over three more times." Turn the packet over. Turn it over again. Then turn it over one more time.

"When you looked at a card, that image became locked in your memory. It is up to me to unlock that memory." As you speak, hold the packet by the ends with the right hand as shown in Figure 13. With the left hand, transfer cards one at a time from the back or bottom to the top of the packet. Continue until you see the card you memorized at the beginning of the trick. In our example, this card is the ♦5.

Do not hesitate or stop after you transfer the ♦5 to the top of the packet. Transfer four more cards, moving them one at a time from the bottom to the top of the packet and say, "I think I found the combination that unlocks your memory. All we have to do is turn the cards over three more times." Turn the packet over, then over again, then over again. Lift the packet so it is vertical. Spread the cards between the hands. Upjog the fourth card from the left, Figure 14.

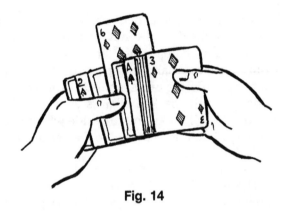

Fig. 14

Remove this card and place it face down on the table. Ask the spectator to name the card he remembered. Turn over the tabled card to show that you were correct.

11. Choices

The magician remarks, "Life is a series of choices. We choose which hobbies to pursue, which job to take, which person to marry. Predictions about future events must also distinguish between the road that will not be taken and the road we choose to take. We're going to track the course of one such journey with these cards."

A shuffled deck is used. The spectator picks two cards. One symbolizes the choice not made and is returned to the deck. The other represents the choice that is made and is memorized by the spectator. This card is also returned to the deck, and the cards are mixed. The spectator then makes another choice as to how many cards will be dealt. This is his secret decision and it is not known to the magician. Nevertheless, the magician correctly predicts the card not chosen as well as the card that was. This trick is based on ideas of Gene Finnell and the author.

Method: Pencil dot the back of a joker, and add this card to a fifty-two-card deck (the trick will work only if the deck contains fifty-three cards). The deck may be used for other tricks. When ready to present "Choices," cut the pencil-dotted card to the top of the deck.

Recite the patter line given above as you push off twenty-six cards from the top of the deck. Do not disturb the order of these cards. The joker is kept on top. Place the twenty-six-card packet aside for the moment, and hand the spectator the balance of the deck. Ask him to shuffle the cards, spread them face down and push two cards out of the packet. "This is your first choice, two cards out of many. Now I'd like you to decide which one of these cards you don't want. Return that card to the packet and give the packet a shuffle."

When the spectator has done this, say, "The remaining card is the card you chose as your card of destiny. Please look at that card and remember it." When the spectator has done this, have him drop the balance of his packet on top of the chosen card. He then places the twenty-seven-card packet on top of the packet that was placed aside earlier. The chosen card is now twenty-seventh from the top of the deck. "I'm going to ask you to make another choice. Please lift off about a third of the deck. Hold onto that packet for the moment."

After the spectator has removed a group of cards, pick up the balance of the deck from above with the right hand. Perform a Klondyke shuffle with this packet by drawing off the top and bottom card simultaneously, and placing this pair on the table, then the next pair of cards, and the next, and so on until you have drawn off the pair that contains the pencil-dotted joker. Drop the remainder of the cards onto the tabled heap. It looks as if you have given the packet a quick shuffle.

There are now two heaps of cards, the one you just mixed and the one cut off by the spectator a moment earlier. Tap the spectator's packet and say, "This is an important choice you made. Your cards will tell us how far to deal." You and the spectator then deal cards simultaneously off the tops of your respective heaps.

Continue until the smaller heap runs out of cards. Point to the top card of your dealt heap. "This is the card we stopped at. I think it's your card. Don't tell us yet which card you chose. I'm going to try to predict which card this is." Pick up a piece of paper and a pen and write "JOKER" on the paper, fold it in half and in half again. Drop it into a teacup. Pick up the top card of your dealt heap and glance at the face as you place it aside. Say this card is the ♦6.

Point to the next top card of the same heap and say, "No, not this one." Toss that card aside. Tap the new top card. "I believe this is the card you chose not to take." On a second piece of paper write, "SIX OF DIAMONDS" (that is, the card you just glimpsed). Fold this paper, but fold it more tightly. Drop it into the teacup and say, "As yet we don't know the identity of either of these cards. The card I thought you didn't choose was . . ." Dump the two pieces of paper out of the teacup. Let them fall to the table. The audience doesn't know which is which. One paper was folded loosely, the other tightly. Pick up the loosely folded piece of paper and open it out to reveal the word "JOKER." Pick up the second card you placed aside and turn it over. It will be the joker.

"Tell us the card you did choose." The spectator will say the ♦6. Open out the other folded paper. It will say, "SIX OF DIAMONDS." Finally, turn over the card first stopped at. It will be the ♦6.

12. Likely Suspect

The magician begins, "At any crime scene, it is more likely than not that the culprit will leave behind clues as a subconscious desire to be caught. A fellow was caught at a poker game while he was in the process of filling a too-perfect hand of draw poker. The fragment of that poker hand has been stored in an evidence locker." The magician then rattles the card box to indicate there are cards inside and continues, "Only the culprit knew which card was needed to complete the hand. You, sir, look like you know your way around a casino. Let's reenact the game." As you speak, remove any ace through 6 in red. The suits are a mixture of hearts and diamonds. Arrange them in numerical order with the ace at the face as shown in Figure 15.

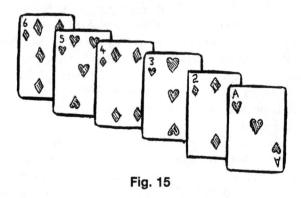

Fig. 15

State that you will also remove the ace through 6 in mixed black suits. With the faces of the cards toward you, remove the ♠A plus the 2 through 6 in red. Do not let the audience see any of the cards you remove from the deck. Arrange them in any order as long as the ♠A is at the face. Already in the card box are the ♠K-♠Q-♠J-♠10.

Turn the "black" packet face down. Drop the face-up red packet on top of it. There is a face-up red ace on top of the combined heap, a face-down ♠A on the bottom. Perform a Klondyke shuffle by drawing the top and bottom card off. (The action of this shuffle is shown in Figure 13 on page 22.) Put this pair on the table. Repeat with the remaining pairs. At the conclusion of the shuffle, a face-up red 6 will be on top of the packet.

Place the packet on the table, and invite the spectator to give it several straight cuts. He continues giving the packet straight cuts until a face-up red card shows on top. Say this card is a red 3. This card is dealt to one side. Invite the spectator to deal the remaining cards into two heaps. He deals the first card at A, the next card at B, the next at C, and so on, as if dealing out two poker hands. There will be a face-up row and a face-down row of cards, Figure 16.

Whatever the value of the card placed aside, the spectator starts at the left end of the face-down row and counts that many cards. In our example, the card placed aside is a red 3. Beginning at the left end of the face-down row, the spectator would count to the third card and turn it over. It will be the ♠A. "Only the guilty party knew that an ace was what was needed to fill the hand."

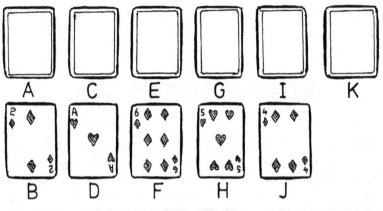

Fig. 16

Turn attention to the card box. Open it and withdraw the cards to show the balance of the Royal Flush in spades.

There is a kicker to the trick. "The other players knew something was wrong because that ace of spades was the only black card in the bunch." Turn up the other cards in the face-down row to show that all of these cards are red.

INTERACTIVE POKER

Interactive games are a popular feature of home computers. They apply to poker tricks as well, with the audience taking an active part in the progress of the game. The five poker tricks in this chapter give the audience the opportunity to participate. This may seem to throw the outcome in doubt, but the magician has things well in control.

13. According to Hoyle

The magician recreates a card game in which a gambler, suspected of cheating, displayed otherworldly skills in winning the hand. The game is five-card stud poker. The magician deals a round of face-down cards, one to each of the five players in the game. Then he deals a face-up card on top of each hole card. One of the players, suspecting trickery, demanded that his face-up card be exchanged with the gambler's. The gambler had no choice but to comply with his request. Here any player exchanges his face-up card with the dealer.

Another round of face-up cards is dealt. One of the other players, claiming that he saw a card come off the bottom, insisted that *both* of his face-up cards be exchanged with the dealer's. Sensing a hostile atmosphere, the gambler had to comply. At this point, the player exchanged his two face-up cards with the dealer's. A third round of cards was dealt out face up. Yet another player cried foul. His *three* face-up cards were exchanged with the dealer's. The fourth and last round of face-up cards was dealt. The gambler appeared hopeful and was about to bet, when the fourth player remarked that he saw the gambler palm a card. There was no alternative but to exchange his four cards with the dealer's.

Remarking that he had been handed all of the losing cards, the dealer invited each player to see what he had been dealt. After their hands were turned face up, the dealer turned his hand face up to reveal that he had the winning hand after all.

Method: A setup does all the work. From the top down the stack is ♥8-♦9-♥4-♣8-♥K-♣4-♣K-♣6-♥7-♦4-♦6-♠7-♥2-♥5-♣9-♦K-♠J-♥3-♥A-♠10-♠Q-♠5-♠K-♥Q-♦2. Place this packet on top of the deck.

When performing poker tricks, it is well to keep in mind that not everyone plays poker. Therefore, one should review the value of the hands for the benefit of the audience. The hands run in order from a pair, two pair, three of a kind, straight, full house, four of a kind, straight flush, to the highest hand, a Royal Flush. Sometimes two players will get, say, a pair of fives. In that case, of the cards remaining in each hand, the player with the highest value card wins.

To present the trick, remark on the fact that you want to replay a game where everyone thought the dealer cheated. Deal the first round face down. Thereafter, on each round, one player exchanges all of his face-up cards with the dealer's face-up cards. Each player is allowed one opportunity to exchange cards, and there must be an exchange on each round for the trick to work. It is of no consequence which player is first to exchange cards with the dealer. No matter what the order of the exchanges, the dealer will hold the winning hand at the close of the game.

To extract maximum entertainment value from the trick, act as if the dealer's chances are rapidly dwindling as more and more cards are taken from him. By the time you reach the final exchange of cards, it should seem as if the dealer has all but given up hope. That he ends up winning the game becomes all that much more of a surprise.

14. Cult Poker

Wizards and warlocks do not play poker by ordinary rules. Since they have the ability to transform any poker hand into a Royal Flush, every game would end in a tie. When wizards play poker it would look like this.

The spectator is given a packet of fourteen cards. She shuffles them and gives seven cards to the magician. The magician shuffles his seven-card hand, withdraws one card and places it into the spectator's poker hand. The spectator shuffles her cards. She is asked to guess which card was placed in her hand by the magician. Whatever card she guesses, she slides that card out and puts it to one side. If it is the correct card, she wins the hand.

The remaining cards in her hand are turned face up. The magician says, "The card I put in your hand was a red five. Remarkably enough, I don't see it here." The spectator turns up the card she placed aside. It is a red 5 and the spectator has won the game.

Method: Beforehand remove the red aces, 3's, 5's and 9's from the deck. Also remove the black 4's, 8's and 10's. Arrange one card of each value in numerical order from ace to 10. The order from the top down will be A-3-4-5-8-9-10. Arrange the other seven cards in reverse numerical order. The order from the top down will be 10-9-8-5-4-3-A. Place one packet on top of the other. Put the combined packet on top of the deck until the time of performance.

To present the trick, push over the top seven cards without disturbing their order, and place them on the table in front of the spectator. Remove the next seven cards without disturbing their order, and place them on the table next to the first packet. Ask the spectator to riffle shuffle the two packets together. After she has done this, ask her to give you the top seven cards. Shuffle these cards, spread them face down on the table and pretend to mull over your choice of cards. Actually, slide any card out of the packet. Glance at the face of this card.

Remember the value of this card. We will assume the card is the ♥9. Slide the ♥9 into the spectator's packet, and invite her to shuffle her cards. She then spreads them face down on the table. Her task is to guess the card you placed in her hand. If she is successful, she has won the game. It does not matter which card she slides out. Put it to one side, and place an object like a book or the card box on top of it to discourage anyone from turning over the card before the trick is over.

The card you placed in her hand is a 9. Silently add nine to forty (the second number is always forty). In this example you will get forty-nine. Remember this total. The spectator's hand contains seven cards. You are going to turn up the cards in her hand to see if your chosen card is still there. Turn up the cards one at a time. As you do, silently add together their values. Assume the cards in the hand are an ace, 3, 4, 8, 9, 9, 10. The total will be forty-four. Subtract this number from your remembered total of forty-nine.

The result will be five. This means that the card placed aside by the spectator is a 5-spot. You do not know the suit of this card but you cover for this by announcing the color. Thus, you say, "This is remarkable. The card I picked was a red five. I don't see it here. If that is the card you placed aside, you win the game!" All that remains is to have someone turn up the card placed aside to prove that it is a red 5.

How do you know the color of the chosen card? You know the color because O-D-D and R-E-D are both spelled with three letters, and all the odd-value cards in the stack are red. So, if the spectator picked an odd-value card, it must be red. If she picked an even-value card, it must be black.

15. Speed Stacking

Gamblers learn how to stack the deck. In a famous poker game run by The Mysterious Kid, the Kid openly stacked the deck so he would get the four aces. Then he decided it would be less suspicious if the aces went to his partner. A spectator decides which spectator will play the part of the magician's partner. He tells no one of his decision, yet the magician succeeds in dealing the aces to the correct hand.

Method: The trick looks like an exhibition of great skill, but it is easy to do. Remove the four aces and a joker from the deck. Turn the deck face down. Reverse the joker so it is face up. Place it on the bottom of the deck and say, "We'll keep the joker reversed on the bottom so the dealer won't be tempted to deal from the bottom of the deck." Spread the deck face down on the table. Openly insert the aces into the deck so they are five cards apart. In other words, the first ace is positioned fifth from the top, the second ace tenth from the top, the third ace fifteenth from the top, and the fourth ace twentieth from the top of the deck.

Square the deck and place it face down on the table. "'The Mysterious Kid' had stacked the deck so he would get the four aces. Then it occurred to him that this was too strong a hand. He was winning steadily anyway. A hand like this would cause the other players to become suspicious. Luckily, he had a partner who was in the game. Sir, I'd like you to think of a number from one to four as an indication of the position of the Kid's partner. Remove that many cards from the top of the deck, but do it silently so I can't know what number you have in mind."

The spectator might decide that the third player is the gambler's partner. He removes three cards from the top of the deck and hides them in his pocket. When he has done this, turn and face the audience. You are going to use the overhand shuffle to restack the cards. Hold the deck in the left hand as shown in Figure 17. The back of the deck is toward the left palm. Grasp the deck by the ends with the right hand. Draw single cards off with the left thumb until you have drawn five cards, one at a time, off the top of the deck and into the left hand. Throw the balance of the deck on top of these five cards.

Fig. 17

Now you are going to repeat the shuffle. Grasp the deck by the ends with the right hand. Draw five more cards off the top one at a time into the left hand, and throw the balance of the deck on top. Repeat this shuffle twice more. When you have finished giving the deck four shuffles, spread the cards until you find the reversed joker. Cut the deck and complete the cut so the joker is back on the bottom. As you perform this shuffle sequence, comment on the fact that "The Mysterious Kid" was attempting the impossible. He was going to restack the aces to fall into a hand that he himself did not know.

After you cut the deck to bring the reversed joker to the bottom, hold the deck in the left hand. Take the top card and bury it in the lower third of the deck. As you do this say, "The top card was buried to keep the game honest." Deal five poker hands of five cards each, dealing a card at a time to each player in turn. Then say to the spectator, "Who did you choose to be the Kid's partner?" In this example, he would say he chose the third player. Turn the other hands face up to show a variety of cards. Then turn the third player's hand face up to show that the kid delivered the aces to the correct hand.

To save time in the performance of this trick, you may wish to secretly stack the aces at every fifth position before the trick begins. Don't tell the audience the cards are stacked. Ask a spectator to secretly remove one to four cards from the top. Stack the deck with the overhand shuffle method described above. When you turn up the hand of the Kid's partner, it will come as a considerable surprise that this hand contains the four aces.

16. Wild Bill's Game

In a game of poker at the Showdown Cafe, Wild Bill removed ten cards from the deck. These were cards of his choice, but he allowed his opponent to pick five of them. Wild Bill would then play with the other five. It looked like a fair game, there was no room for cheating, but Wild Bill wouldn't play in a game where he couldn't cheat. No matter which five cards his opponent took, Wild Bill always came out a winner.

Method: The trick is impromptu and can be done with any deck. The cards are set up as the patter story is related. "Wild Bill removed a bunch of interesting cards from the deck for the final round of poker on a night when he wasn't winning a lot of money. This was going to be the last hand of the night, double or nothing." As you speak those lines remove the following ten cards from the deck. Arrange them in the order shown in Figure 18-A, i.e., 7-7-9-9-J-J-10-10-Q-8.

The top card of the packet is a 7-spot. The bottom card is an 8. Continue, "Wild Bill picked the ten cards he and his opponent would play with, but his opponent got to choose which five of those cards would be in his hand." Take the top two cards with the right hand. The spectator who plays the part of your opponent takes either

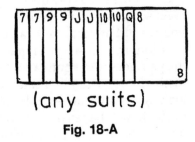

(any suits)

Fig. 18-A

card sight unseen and places it on the table before him. Spread the cards in the left hand so that the bottom card is slightly exposed. The card not chosen by the spectator is slid between the bottom two cards as shown in Figure 18-B. As you do this say, "We'll get rid of the card you don't want." Square up the packet.

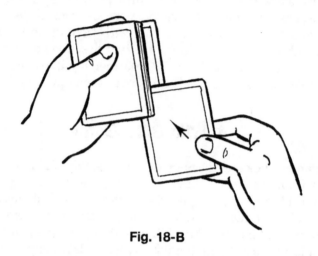

Fig. 18-B

Take the next two cards with the right hand. The spectator picks one of them. Place the unwanted card on the bottom of the packet. Proceed in like manner with the third and fourth pairs of cards. In each case the unwanted card goes on the bottom. When you get to the fifth pair, turn up the top card of this pair. It will be a queen. Say, "Wild Bill wanted to give his opponent a sporting chance, so he said, 'This is the only queen in the game and it is the highest of the ten cards in play.' Wild Bill could have said this to persuade you to take the queen, or he might want you to be suspicious of an offer that sounds too good to be true. It's your choice. Take either the queen or the other card."

As soon as the spectator makes his choice, say, "Are you sure you want that card? You can change your mind." Whatever his decision, the chosen card goes into his hand. The other card of the pair goes into your hand. "Remember that a pair, two pair or three of a kind can be beaten by a straight, and every player is looking for that unbeatable hand." Turn up his cards one at a time. He will have either a broken straight or a pair of 7's. Turn up your hand to reveal a winning straight.

17. The New Deal

If you wish to repeat Wild Bill's Game, but under more stringent conditions, this trick fills the bill. Ten cards are removed from the deck and given to the spectator. He shuffles the cards any way he likes and deals two poker hands, one to himself, one to the magician. The magician says, "Look at the face of one card in your hand. If you think you can improve things by getting rid of this card, exchange it with any card in my hand. Of course, you can't look at my hand when you do this."

The spectator may or may not elect to change this card with any card in the magician's hand. After he has made his decision, the magician says to him, "Look at the face of any other card in your hand. Again you have the option of exchanging this card for any card in my hand. As before, you can't look at my cards when you do this."

After the spectator has been given this second opportunity, the magician says, "The dealer also gets a turn, but only one. Mix up my cards. I'll turn my back while you do this so I can't know where any card is." The spectator mixes the magician's cards. "Now it's my turn." The magician exchanges one card from his hand with one card from the spectator's hand. When the two poker hands are turned up, it is seen that the magician has the better hand.

Method: This trick exploits a gambler's method of getting the winning hand. You must use your own cards because some small preparation is involved, but the trick can be done at any time during the performance. Pencil dot the back of a card, Figure 19, so you can recognize the card from the back. Say the card is the ♣3. This completes the preparation.

To perform the trick, upjog three 2's, three 5's, three 6's and the ♣3. Strip these ten cards out of the deck, and place the rest of the deck aside. Hand the ten cards to the spectator. Invite him to shuffle them any way he likes and deal out two poker hands, one to himself, one to you. Explain that in a

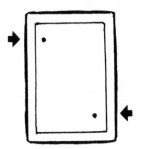

Fig. 19

famous card game played between millionaires at the Waldorf Astoria not too long ago, each player wanted to be certain he got the maximum chance to win. The opponents hit on the following scheme.

The spectator picks one of his cards, looks at it and decides whether he wants this card or he thinks you should have it. Say to him, "Of course you can't look at my hand. But you can take any card in exchange. If your card is a particularly low-value card, you may decide it would look better in my hand." His decision has no bearing on the outcome of the game. Let's say he decides to exchange his card with one of yours.

Continue, "Just to make the game completely fair, please look at another card in your hand. You have the same opportunity. If you think that card is a good one to hold onto, keep it for yourself. Otherwise, you can exchange it for any card in my hand." The spectator can keep the card or he can exchange it. After he has been given two opportunities to make exchanges, it is your turn. First check the position of the pencil-dotted card. If it is in the spectator's hand, simply turn the two poker hands face up. You will have the winning hand.

If the pencil-dotted card is in your hand, say, "You were given two chances to better your hand. The dealer is given one. Just to make absolutely sure I won't cheat, I'm going to turn my head aside. Please mix up the cards in my hand." When the spectator has done this, turn and face him. Exchange the pencil-dotted card for any card in his hand. Have the two poker hands turned face up to reveal that you hold the winning hand.

RED–BLACK TRICKS

The tricks in this chapter make use of the fact that playing cards are either red or black. This simple feature of playing cards is exploited for use in prediction tricks, betting games and revelations.

18. Color of Thought

When you wish to perform a prediction effect with a borrowed deck of cards, this trick can be done at any time. The magician writes a prediction and puts it to one side. A borrowed deck is then divided into two heaps. The top half is given to the spectator who shuffles it and counts the number of red cards in that half of the deck. Say he counts ten reds.

The magician tells him that he will count to the tenth *black* card in the other half of the deck. "Since red attracts black," he says, "it will be interesting to see what the tenth black card looks like." There are no false moves. He counts to the tenth black card in the other half of the deck. It could be the ♠8. The prediction is opened by a spectator. It says, "YOU WILL CHOOSE THE EIGHT OF SPADES."

Method: The deck must contain the full fifty-two cards and no jokers. When the deck is handed to you, spread the cards between the hands so you can see the faces. Remember the black card nearest the face of the deck. Say this card is the ♠8. Close up the deck and place it on the table. On a piece of paper write, "YOU WILL CHOOSE THE EIGHT OF SPADES." Fold the paper and place it to one side. Usually, I will place it in the card case, close the flap and hand the card case to someone to hold.

Pick up the deck, count off the top twenty-six cards and hand them to the spectator. Direct him to shuffle them. He is then to count the number of red cards in his packet. Say he counts ten reds. Say, "On the theory that red attracts black, I'm going to count to the tenth *black* card in the other half of the deck." You are holding the packet face down in the left hand. Take the top card of your packet with the right hand, and turn it face up to see if it is black. If so, count "one." If it isn't, say nothing. In either case, transfer this card to the bottom of the packet. Continue this way until you have counted to the tenth black card. It will be the ♠8. Have the prediction opened and read aloud to verify that you were able to correctly see into the future.

If the preceding effect was well received, you are in a position to perform an offbeat follow-up trick. Replace the ♠8 on top of your packet. Invite the spectator to shuffle his packet and drop it back on top of the deck. While you turn your head to one side, ask him to cut a small packet (no more than fifteen cards) off the top of the deck. Direct him to silently count the number of reds in the packet. Then he is to hide the packet in his pocket. Say he counted six reds. He does not tell you this number. Whatever the number, he looks at the card at that position from the top of the deck. In our example, he would look at and remember the card that is sixth from the top.

Turn around and face the audience. Lift up the top two-thirds of the deck. The number of cards is not important as long as the packet contains the prediction card from the previous trick—the ♠8 in our example. You are going to do a neat bit of figuring to find out the card chosen by the spectator. First, count the number of red cards above the ♠8. Say you count four. You know from the previous trick that there were ten reds in the spectator's packet originally. Since there are only four, he must have the other six in his pocket. This means that he looked at the sixth card from the top of the deck. Count to the sixth card from the top of your packet. It will be the chosen card.

19. Card Roulette

The magician remarks, "Most people lose most of the time when they play their lucky number. The reason is well known to scientists who study these things. Your number is indeed lucky, but most of the time it is lucky for somebody else. In the lab, this is demonstrated with a game called 'card roulette.'"

As you speak, remove a pair of aces from the deck such that the leftmost ace is red and the rightmost ace is black. Place the pair of aces face down on the table. The red ace is the uppermost of the two cards. Following the same rule, remove a pair of 2's (the leftmost two is red, the rightmost two black). Place this pair on top of the pair of aces. Repeat with a pair of 3's, a pair of 4's, and so on through a pair of 7's. The colors will alternate red-black-red-black from top to bottom. The topmost card of the fourteen-card packet will be a red 7. The bottom card is a black ace.

Hold the packet face down in the left hand. "First we're going to pick some lucky cards. Just say 'stop' as I transfer cards from top to bottom." Push off the top pair of cards and place them on the bottom of the packet without disturbing the order of these two cards. Transfer the next pair and the next, and so on until the spectator calls "stop." It does not matter when "stop" is called. Hand the top card of the packet to a spectator on the left. Hand the next card to a spectator on the right. These two cards will be of the same value but opposite color. Ask each person to remember his card.

Take back the card from the spectator on the left and place it on top of the packet. Take back the card from the spectator on the right and place it on top. "Just so we can verify your choices later on, please jot down the names of your lucky cards." Hand the spectators paper and pen to record their choices. The reason you do this is to afford yourself a time delay. The audience knows the chosen cards are on top, but you don't want them to know exactly which card is which.

Deal the packet into two heaps, dealing from left to right a card at a time until all cards have been dealt. Pick up the heap on the left, and say to the spectator on the left, "Sir, I'd like you to pick a lucky number. We have only seven cards here, so please choose a number between one and seven." The spectator can choose any number so long as it is not one or seven. Say he picks four. You reply, "Good. We're going to play card roulette. The croupier will allow six chances for your lucky card to come up. We will use the number four each time."

Transfer three cards from the top to bottom of the packet, saying "One, two, three" aloud as you do so. When you get to the fourth card, pause with the fourth card in hand and say, "Four. Is this your card?" Turn it face up. The spectator will say no. Place this card, still face up, on the bottom of the packet.

Repeat the process five more times. Each time the spectator's card will not show. After the sixth round say, "You can see what they mean. The player is given six chances out of seven and his card does not show up." The principle that makes this trick work was invented by George Sands. It guarantees that the chosen card will not show up in six tries, no matter which number the spectator chooses.

Place the packet on the table in a spread condition. There will be six face-up red cards and one face-down card. The audience assumes this is the chosen red card. Pick up the other packet. Ask the second spectator for a different number between one and seven. Say the number is three. Deal each of the top two cards to the bottom of the second packet, saying "One, two," as you deal. Pause when you get to the third card. Turn it face up and say, "Is this your card?" The second spectator says no. Place the face-up card under the packet.

Repeat this routine five more times with the second spectator. The chosen card does not show up. You now have two packets of face-up cards on the table. One is all red with a face-down card. The other is all black with a face-down card. Point to the all-red packet, and say to the first spectator, "Your number was lucky, but it was lucky for *his* card." Take the face-down card and turn it over to show it is the black card chosen by the second spectator. Repeat with the other packet. The face-down card in the black packet is the red card chosen by the first spectator.

20. Flip Over Mystery

Without showing the audience the faces of the cards, remove any black card from the deck and place it face down on the table. Remove any red card and place it to the right of the first card. Continue in this fashion until you have constructed the sixteen-card layout shown in Figure 20.

Ask the spectator to pick any card. Whatever card he chooses, pick a card for yourself that is either to the right or left of his card in the same row. This means that if he chooses a red card, you will choose a black, and vice versa. Take his card and place it

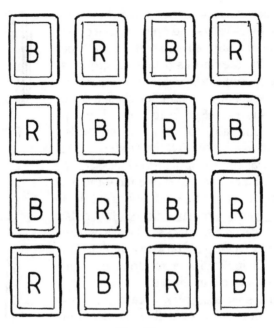

Fig. 20

back in the blank space occupied by *your* card. Place your card in the blank space occupied by his card. Next ask the spectator to gather the cards by starting at any card and flipping it over onto the card next to it, Figure 21. Then he flips these two cards over onto the next card. The flip-over process is done horizontally or vertically. He can start at any card, and he can take any path he chooses as the cards are gathered. Each time, the packet must be flipped over onto the next card. If there is a blank space separating the packet from the next card, he flips it over onto the blank space, Figure 22, and then flips it over again onto the card.

It would appear that the cards are in a haphazard arrangement, but that is not true. There will be two groups of cards, one face up

Fig. 21

and one face down. Further, one group will contain all black cards and one red. The other group will contain all red cards and one black. Finally, the odd card in each group is one of the chosen cards.

Ask the spectator to name his chosen card. He might say the ♠8. Spread the red group face up on the table to reveal all red cards, and one black—the ♠8. Tell the audience that your card was the ♦3. Spread the black group to show all black cards and one red—the ♦3. The arrangement can be made more subtle if odd-value cards are substituted for reds, even-value cards for blacks. The cards can then be dealt face-up in the array depicted in Figure 20. It looks like a random arrangement of cards to the audience.

Have the spectator pick a card. Say his card is an odd-value card like the ♠5. You then choose any even-value card like the ♦2. Put his card back in the blank space formerly occupied by your card. Put your card back in the other blank space. Ask him to gather the

Fig. 22

cards by the seemingly random procedure described on the previous page. Then reveal that the odd cards have somehow gathered themselves in one heap, the even cards in the other. Further, the one card that does not belong in each heap is a chosen card.

21. Center Vision

Some card effects can be performed under strict test conditions that seem to prevent trickery. In this trick, the spectator shuffles the deck. He is asked to remember the card that is exactly twenty-sixth from the top. The magician points out that if he wanted to find the spectator's card, all he would have to do is count to the twenty-sixth card. To get away from the idea of counting, the spectator hands the magician the middle third of the deck. Studying just these few cards, the magician reveals the card chosen by the spectator.

Using the same shuffled deck, the effect is repeated, though with a difference. The spectator is asked to remember the card that is exactly tenth from the face of the deck. When he has done this, the magician is handed about two-thirds of the deck. He deals cards off the top one at a time. Then he stops and says, "I get the impression that I am getting close to your card. In fact, it is exactly three down from the top." The spectator then deals three cards off the top. The third card is indeed the chosen pasteboard.

Method: The deck is going to be stacked ahead of time in a simple red–black setup. This would seem to be of no value since the spectator is going to give the deck a genuine shuffle. But a crucial piece of information will survive the shuffle and allow you to perform both of the tricks.

Separate reds from blacks. Stack all the reds in the top half of the deck in random order, but make sure the ♥A is thirteenth from the top of the red group. Stack all the blacks in the bottom half of the deck in random order, but make sure the ♠A is thirteenth from the top of the black group.

When you are ready to perform the trick, split the deck at the midpoint. Place the two halves on the table in front of the spectator. Ask him to riffle shuffle the two halves together. Turn your head to one side, and ask the spectator to hold the shuffled deck in his left hand. He is to deal cards off the top into a face-up heap on the table. When he deals the twenty-sixth card, he is to remember this card.

When he has dealt to the twenty-sixth card, there will be a face-up packet on the table. The face card of this packet is his card. Ask him to turn the packet face down and drop it on top of the balance of the deck. He is then to place the deck on the table. Remark that it would be easy for you to find his card. All you have to do is count to the twenty-sixth card. To test your ability to find a card under genuine test conditions, it must be impossible for you to use this ruse. Accordingly, ask the spectator to cut the deck into three heaps. The heaps should be approximately equal. When he has done this, pick up the center heap. His card is in this heap, but you don't as yet know where. You are going to look through this heap and toss out his card. It is done as follows.

Spread the cards in the center heap so you alone can see the faces. Look for the ♥A and the ♠A. There are three possibilities.

(a) These two aces are adjacent to one another. In this case, the leftmost ace is twenty-sixth from the top of the deck. This is the chosen card. Toss it face down on the table. Ask that the chosen card be named. Then turn the ace face up.

(b) The ♥A is several cards to the left of the ♠A. In this case, count the number of black cards between the ♥A and the ♠A. Subtract this number from twenty-five. Whatever the result, that number is the position of the ♥A from the top of the deck. For example, you see that the ♥A is to the left of the ♠A, and that there are five black cards between the ♥A and the ♠A. Subtract five from twenty-five to get twenty. This tells you that the ♥A would be twentieth from the top if the deck was reassembled. Count six cards to the right of the ♥A to arrive at the twenty-sixth card, the one chosen by the spectator.

(c) The ♥A is several cards to the right of the ♠A. Count the number of black cards between the ♥A and the ♠A. Add that number to twenty-six. Whatever the result, that number is the position of the ♥A from the top of the deck. For example, you see that the ♥A is to the right of the ♠A, and that there are four black cards between these two aces. Add four to twenty-six to arrive at thirty. This tells you that the ♥A would be thirtieth from the top if the deck was reassembled. Count four cards back to the left from the ♥A, and that is the spectator's card.

To perform the second effect, assemble the deck so it is back in order. In other words, put the top third on top of the middle third, and this combined packet on top of the bottom third. Turn your head to one side. Ask the spectator to turn the deck face up and deal a heap of ten cards to the table. The rest of the deck is then placed face up on the table. Invite him to shuffle the ten cards and take one. He is to remember this card.

Ask him to place the chosen card onto the face of the larger packet. Then he places the balance of the cards in hand onto the face of the deck. His card is now tenth from the face of the deck. Finally, direct him to turn the deck face down on the table. Now, turn and face him and say, "Once again, I could merely count to your card. To prevent that from happening, please cut off about a third of the deck from the top. Place this packet to one side. Your card is now at a random location from the top of this packet."

Deal cards one at a time from the top of the large packet into a

face-up heap on the table. Continue dealing until you reach the
♥A. From the previous effect, you know the exact location of the
♥A from the top of the deck. If it was twenty-third, then when
you reach the ♥A, twenty-three becomes the first number in your
count. Turn your head to one side, and deal cards off the top of
the tabled packet into a face-up heap on the table. Silently
advance in the count until you reach forty. Stop and say, "I am
getting a sense that I am near your card. In fact, your card is
exactly third down." (It is always third down from the fortieth
card.) Ask the spectator to name his card. He then deals to the
third card down and it will be his card.

22. Backwards Bet

The magician begins, "Usually people bet that they will guess
right. This game is played backwards. If I guess right, I'll pay you
a dollar. If I'm wrong, I keep the money. I want you to have a fair
run for my money, so we'll play four rounds." The spectator
shuffles the deck and has a free choice of the cards that are used.
No matter how hard he tries, the magician can't give away his
money.

Method: The deck is secretly set up according to color. Have
two reds on top, then two blacks, then two reds, then two blacks,
and so on, the colors arranged in pairs and the colors alternating
in this fashion throughout the deck. When you have arranged the
cards in this way, transfer the bottom black card to the top of the
deck. There is now a black card on top and bottom.

When ready to perform this bet, split the deck in the middle
between two adjacent black cards. Place the two halves of the
deck on the table in front of the spectator. Invite him to riffle
shuffle the two halves together. He performs the shuffle just
once. Take the shuffled deck from him. Remark that you are
going to use groups of four cards, but that he will decide which
groups are used. Push the top four cards off the deck. Ask if he
wants these four cards. If he says yes, drop them onto the table.
If he says no, transfer them to the bottom of the deck. Continue
in this manner until you have four four-card groups on the table.
Place the remainder of the deck aside.

Pick up one of the four-card groups. Deal the top two cards off and turn them face up. The two cards might be two reds. "You shuffled the deck and you decided which cards we would use. Those two cards are red. These other two cards can both be black, they can both be red, or they can be one of each color. It's all a matter of chance, and the odds are against me, but I'll bet a dollar that these two cards are both black." The two cards are turned face up. Both are black.

How do you know? The system is simple. If the first two cards are the same color, the other two will both be of the opposite color. If the two cards you turn face up are a red and a black, then the other two cards will be a red and a black. But don't make it seem this simple. Ponder the situation. Remind the spectator that he shuffled and he decided which groups of four you would use. Then have him point to another group of four cards. Deal the top two cards to the table. Turn one of them face up and say, "Before I turn the other card of this pair face up, maybe you would like to change your mind. Maybe you want the two cards of the other pair instead."

It doesn't matter. If the first pair contains matching colors, the second pair will contain two matching cards of the opposite color. If the cards in the first pair don't match, the cards in the second pair won't either. On the third round, you can vary things still further. Have him choose one of the remaining two groups of four cards. Deal the top two cards face down to the table. Ask him if he wants to exchange one card of this pair with one card of the other pair. Turn your head to one side while he does this. Turn up the first pair. Follow the above system to reveal whether the second pair matches or not.

On the final round, act discouraged that you can't give away your money. Hand him all four cards. Direct him to shuffle them and take two sight unseen. He gives you the other two cards. Ask him to decide who turns his cards face up. As before, it doesn't matter. As soon as you see the faces of the cards in one pair, you know the colors of the cards in the other pair.

23. Blackgammon

Stores that cater to coin collectors will sometimes have for sale odd or unusual foreign coins that can be obtained at a small price. It is worthwhile to purchase one or two such coins. They can be used in tricks like the following, where magical powers are seemingly granted to the spectator.

An odd coin is displayed. It is said to contain a spell that allows someone to temporarily gain unusual powers. To test the strength of the coin's power, the magician sets up a test. He removes an assortment of red cards and black cards from the deck, and openly arranges them into two heaps. One heap is placed face-to-face with the other. This means that no matter which side is up, a back will show.

The coin is slid over toward the spectator. She is asked to touch it for a moment to increase her sensitivity to color. She is then asked to turn the packet over several times and take the top card. This card is placed face down on the table in front of her. No one knows the identity of this card. The packet is then handed to the magician. He turns the packet over several times and takes the top card. This too is a card whose identity is unknown. The packet is handed back to the lady. She turns the packet over and over, and then she takes the top card. The packet is handed to the performer, who follows the same procedure.

The process continues for several more cards. The lady goes first on each round and has an absolutely free choice. No one knows the identity of any card she picks. At the finish, each person will have some cards. The magician says, "The power of this coin is such that it makes your fingertips sensitive to the color red. I have been denied this power, so the result of my choices is not surprising." He turns over his cards. They are a mixture of red and black cards.

"The result with your cards should be quite different." The lady turns over her cards. *All* of her cards are red.

Method: Stack eight cards in the color order, red-black-red-black-red-red-red-black. Suits and values do not matter, but you should use a mixture so that the cards appear to be randomly ordered. Arrange a second group of eight cards in the same order. Place one packet face up on the table. Place the other packet face down on top of it.

Remove the odd-looking coin from the pocket. If a coin is not readily available, use an antique finger ring, which you claim belonged to a witch. Slide it in the direction of the volunteer. Ask her to touch it in order to effect the transfer of power. Then turn the packet over and over, and hand it to the spectator. Ask her to turn the packet over several times. She then deals the top card to herself. Take the remainder of the packet. Turn it over an even number of times, and then take the top card. Repeat the process several times. The only rule is that the spectator must take a face-down card. You will eventually run out of cards on one side. When this happens, the experiment is over.

Call attention to your cards. Remark that without the power of the coin, you can do no better than chance. Turn over your cards to show a mixture of reds and blacks. Due to the power of the coin to perceive the color red, the lady will achieve far different results. She turns over her cards to reveal that all of her cards are red.

MARKED FOR MYSTERY

Magic tricks are conveniently divided into two parts, effect and method. The effect is the trick that is seen by the audience. The method is the same trick from the magician's perspective. The difference is that more happens in terms of method than is known to the audience. To say it another way, the method allows the magician to move ahead of the audience so that more is accomplished than meets the eye. Marked cards are one of the tricks of the magician's trade. They give the magician secret information that allows him to stay ahead of the game. Professionally marked decks are available from magic supply shops. In this chapter, we will exploit the situation where a single card is secretly marked.

24. Stop or Else!

Essentially, this trick involves the surprise location of a chosen card when the pack is out of your hands. The preparation consists of writing the word "STOP!" (or, more forcefully, "STOP OR ELSE!") on the face of a joker, Figure 23. Turn the joker face down. Place a light pencil dot on diagonally opposite corners of the joker, Figure 24, so you can identify this card later on.

Fig. 23

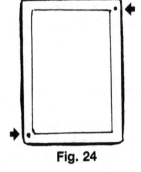

Fig. 24

Leave the joker in the card case when you remove the deck. Perform other tricks, then remark that you want to make use of the joker for a special trick. Keep the joker face down as you remove it from the card case. Don't show the face of this card, and position it twenty-seventh from the top of the deck. I do this by fanning the cards from left to right so I can see the faces. I count from the left end of the fan until the twenty-sixth card is reached. The joker is then inserted into the fan to the right of this card.

The joker must be exactly twenty-seventh from the top for the trick to work, but I use an offhand bit of business that makes it seem as if the location of the joker is not important. The deck is held in the left hand. As I talk about the special powers of the joker, I remove a packet of about a dozen cards from the top of the deck with the right hand, Figure 25. Then the left thumb riffles off the top seven or eight cards of the packet in the left hand.

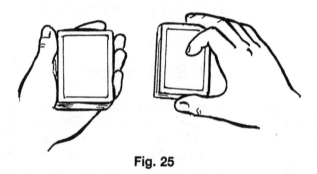

Fig. 25

At the same time, the right hand changes its grip slightly. The packet is clipped between the right first and second fingers. The right thumb releases its grip. The packet is then inserted into the break established by the left thumb as shown in Figure 26. This looks like a casual cut of the deck, but really it involves only the top few cards. The joker is still twenty-seventh down from the top.

Turn your head to one side. Ask the spectator to think of any number from one to ten. He deals two heaps, each containing the chosen number. Ask him to look at the face (or bottom) card of one heap. He places that heap on top of the deck, and the deck is then placed on top of the other heap. Now, turn and face the spectator. Ask him to deal a heap of thirteen cards on the table. When he has done this, ask him to deal a second heap. Wait for the pencil-dotted joker to be dealt. Then tell the spectator he can stop at any time.

It does not matter how many cards he deals. When he has finished dealing the second heap, turn this heap face up. Place it alongside the first heap, and instruct

Fig. 26

the spectator to simultaneously deal cards off both heaps. That is, he deals the top card of the face-down heap with one hand, and the top card of the face-up heap with the other hand. Say, "The joker will give you a subtle hint when you have dealt enough cards." The "subtle hint" is delivered when the spectator reaches the joker. It commands him to "STOP OR ELSE!" "I know you didn't pick the joker," the magician says. "What card did you pick?" When the spectator names his card, direct him to turn over the top card of the face-down packet. It will be his card.

In Figure 24, the mark is shown at the white border of the card. The mark is better concealed if it is placed within the back pattern. Use a red pencil to mark a red-backed card, a blue pencil to mark a blue-backed card. The marks should be large enough for you to spot easily, but not so large that they can be spotted by the audience. If you wish to perform a similar trick on a later occasion, "Back Stop," the first trick in the chapter "Novelty Tricks," is another good candidate.

25. Metal with Memory

A pencil-dotted card is used in this trick to simplify the handling. The effect was invented by Howard Adams. The magician recounts a poker game where a penny, nickel, and dime were used as betting units. In the game they represented $1 million, $5 million, and $10 million respectively. The winning player held three aces. Oddly enough, the coins seemed to remember the outcome of the game and could duplicate it at any time.

The spectator arranges the three coins in a row in any order he likes. Let's say he arranges them in the order nickel-penny-dime. Beginning at the left end of the row, the magician deals five cards next to the nickel, one card next to the penny, and ten cards next to the dime, as shown in Figure 27. The top card of each heap is turned up. Each card is an ace. The order of the coins does not matter. The outcome is always the same.

Method: This solution makes use of the ideas of Frank Thompson, Mel Bennett and Stewart James. Pencil dot the back of a joker. Arrange the four aces and the joker as follows. An ace is on top of the deck. Another ace is sixth from the top. Another ace is eleventh from the top. The marked joker is fifteenth from the top. The last ace is sixteenth from the top.

Recount the story of the poker game. "The bets were in millions. I left my cash box at home, so we will use these coins instead." Toss a penny, nickel, and dime to the table. The spectator arranges them in a row in any order, say nickel-penny-dime. Beginning with the coin at the far left end of the row (the nickel), deal five cards in a heap next to it. Deal one card next to the penny. Deal a heap of ten cards next to the dime. The layout looks like Figure 27.

There are two ways the trick can end. The pencil-dotted card tells you which ending to use. If the top card of the middle heap has no pencil dot, turn over the heap on the left to show an ace.

Fig. 27

Then grasp the top card of each of the other heaps, one in each hand, and simultaneously turn them over to show the second and third aces. The only other possibility is that the top card of the center heap has the pencil-dotted card on top. In that case, turn over the top card of the rightmost heap. Then grasp each of the other two heaps, one in each hand, and simultaneously turn them over to show the second and third aces.

As the trick is done, comment that the coins seemed to retain a memory of the card game, and had no trouble duplicating the outcome.

26. Cutting the Aces

Sleight-of-hand experts are expected to be able to cut to the four aces. It would be surprising if this rare skill could be temporarily transferred to a spectator. This premise for a card trick was suggested by William P. Miesel. I devised an easy method for performing it.

Beforehand, pencil dot the back of a joker. Place the black aces on either side of the joker. Put this three-card group in the middle of the deck. Place one red ace on top of the deck and one on the bottom. The setup is as shown in Figure 28.

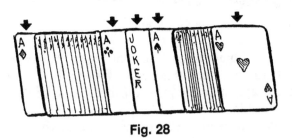

Fig. 28

Other tricks may be performed with the deck as long as the setup is not disturbed. For example, one can remove the four queens from the deck and perform No. 36, "Greeks Bearing Gifts" from the chapter "Mind Reading." Place the queens aside after the performance of that trick and go on with "Cutting the Aces."

Fig. 29

To perform the trick, spread the cards from left to right between the hands. Spot the pencil-dotted joker, and separate the deck so that the joker is the bottom card of the left-hand packet. As you do this say, "With your help, I'd like to divide the deck into four heaps." Place the two halves of the deck alongside one another on the table. Turn the left heap face up, Figure 29. Pretending that the presence of the joker is an accident, say, "I'll get rid of the joker in a moment. But first, do me a favor. Lift off half of the left heap and place it to the left of that heap. At the same time, lift off half of the right heap and place it to the right of that heap." When the spectator has done this, flip the end heaps over. The result is that you have four heaps on the table as shown in Figure 30.

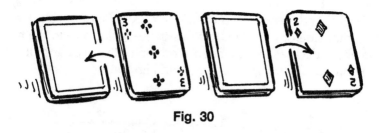

Fig. 30

"Let's get rid of that joker." Grasp the leftmost heap from above with the left hand. Keep this heap parallel with the table. With the right fingers, slide the joker off the bottom of the heap and toss it to one side.

"Now we can begin. Let's see what cards you cut to." Still holding the leftmost heap with the left hand, slide the bottom card out and drop it on the table in front of you. This card is the ♣A, but don't show it. Place the heap on the table, and pick up the next heap with the left hand. This is the heap with the ♣3 on the face. "We'll take the back card of this heap also." Lift the heap so the back of the cards faces the audience, Figure 31. Slide the back card out with the right fingers, Figure 32. Grasp this card (an ace) with the right thumb and forefinger. Turn the right hand palm down and drop this card on top of the ♣A. Replace the packet face-up in its original location on the table.

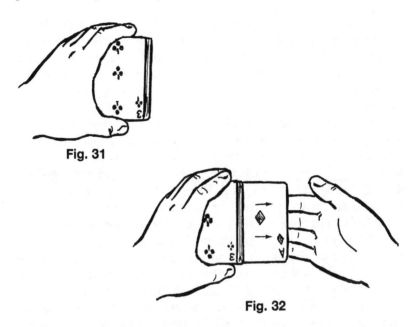

Fig. 31

Fig. 32

Pick up the next heap with the left hand, and keep it horizontal (parallel with the table top). Slide the bottom card out. This card is the ♥A. Drop it onto the ace heap. Replace the packet face down on the table. The rightmost heap is the last heap. Grasp it from above with the left hand. Lift the packet to a vertical position as in Figure 31. Slide the backmost card out, Figure 32. It will be the ♠A. As with the other aces, don't show the face of this card. Turn the right hand palm down and drop the ♠A face down on top of the other aces. Replace the packet on the table.

"You divided the deck into four heaps." Tap the ace packet. "We have a record of the cards you cut to." As you speak, turn the face-up heaps face down. There are now four face-down heaps on the table. "Sometimes people are temporarily endowed with the ability to control the cards like an expert." Pick up the ace packet and hold it face down in the left hand. Take the top ace, turn it face up and drop it onto one of the packets. Repeat with the other aces. Congratulate the spectator on the amazing outcome.

27. Scrambled Stud

Among card players, five-card stud poker is considered to be one of the games that requires a high level of skill. Most of the cards in a stud poker hand are face up, but the hole card is face down. A seasoned gambler can make a shrewd guess as to the identity of the other fellow's hole card. This trick shows how it is done.

Before performing the trick, lightly pencil dot the back of the ♥K so that you can recognize this card later on. This preparation does not interfere with other tricks you may want to perform with the deck. Ten court cards are stacked in the order ♥K-♠J-♥Q-♠K-♣Q-♦K-♣J-♦Q-♣K-♣Q. The ♥K is the top card. The ♣Q is the bottom card of the packet. The setup for the ten cards can be done in front of the audience. As you arrange the cards, comment that these cards represent strong hands in the game of stud poker. Close up the stack and turn the packet face down. Give the packet several straight cuts. When you cut the cards for the last time, cut the pencil-dotted ♥K to the bottom of the packet.

Hand the packet to the spectator, and turn your head to one side. Say to him, "Gamblers study the psychology of card players so they can make educated guesses about a player's hole card in a game of stud poker. I'd like you to spread the cards so you can see the faces. Think of any club or diamond. Don't tell me which one. Jot down the card you're thinking of on a piece of paper. I'm not going to touch the paper. We're just going to use it for later verification. Have you done that? Good. I'd also like you to jot down the position of the card from the top of the packet. It could be fifth or ninth or whatever. Just jot down its position."

The chosen card may be the ♣J. It is sixth from the top of the packet. Of course, you do not know this. When the writing has been done, ask the spectator to close up the packet and give it several straight cuts to mix the cards. Then say, "Every card in that packet has a card of the same value and color but the opposite suit. In other words, if your card is, say, the queen of clubs, the queen of the same color and opposite suit would be the queen of spades. Hold the packet face up so you can see the cards. Find the card that has the same value and color as your card, but has the opposite suit. Cut that card to the face or bottom of the packet."

The spectator's first card may have been the ♣J. The card that is opposite to this one is the ♠J. He cuts the ♠J to the face of the packet. When he has done this, ask him to concentrate on this card. Then direct him to turn the packet face down. Whatever position was occupied by the first card, he is now to transfer that many cards, one at a time, from the top to the bottom of the packet. In our example, he would transfer six cards, one at a time, from top to bottom. As before, your head is turned to one side. You do not know how many cards were transferred.

Take the packet from the spectator, and don't look at the faces of the cards. Spread the cards with the faces toward the spectator. "You picked two hole cards merely by thinking of them. It's up to the gambler to figure out which cards they were." As you speak, note the position of the pencil-dotted card from the top of the packet. In Figure 33, it is third from the top. You are going to do a simple bit of figuring that will reveal the location of the cards thought of by the spectator.

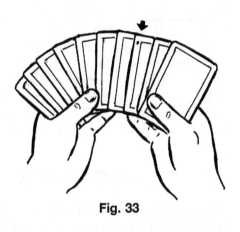

Fig. 33

Whatever the position of the pencil-dotted card, add five to it and divide the result by two. In our example, the ♥K is third from the top. Three plus five is eight, and eight divided by two is four. Square up the packet. Transfer four cards one at a time from top to bottom as you say, "We'll just mix them up a bit." Deal the top four cards face up to the spectator. Deal the next card face down. Deal the next four cards face up to your hand, and the last card face down. Say, "Just by analyzing body language and other subconscious factors, I'd guess that you were thinking of the black jacks as hole cards." Name the cards that are not shown among the face-up cards. The spectator must agree that you are correct.

In the performance of this trick, one of the spectator's thought cards will always be among the top five cards of the packet. When you perform the figuring given above, if you get a number higher than five, deduct five and use that number. For example, the spectator thinks of the ♣K. It is eighth from the top of the packet. He cuts the ♠K to the face of the packet. Then he turns the packet face down and transfers eight cards from top to bottom.

When you spread the cards face down, you see that the pencil-dotted ♥K is ninth from the top of the packet. Nine plus five is fourteen, and half of that is seven. This number is greater than five, so five is deducted, reducing the result to two. Transfer two cards from top to bottom. Deal the top four cards face up to the spectator. Deal the next card face down to him. You have five cards left. Deal the first four cards face up to your hand and the last card face down. Note which cards don't show among the face-up cards. In this example, the black kings don't show. Remark that you sized up the spectator, and came to the conclusion that he would think of the ♣K and the ♠K.

This trick is based on an idea of Bob Hummer's. It falls into the category of tricks based on a minimum amount of information. In this case, the position of a pencil-dotted card reveals the location of each of two cards merely thought of by the spectator. The fact that you never see the faces of the cards adds to the mystery.

28. Conceal and Reveal

Charles Jordan invented an ingenious way to reveal a card chosen in a fair way by a spectator. This trick builds on Jordan's premise. With the deck in his own hands, a spectator lifts off about half, looks at the card cut to, and replaces the cut portion. The deck is given several straight cuts to mix the cards. Then a second and a third spectator look at cards in a similar manner. Without asking a single question, the magician reveals each of the chosen cards.

Method: It is necessary to secretly prepare one card by placing a short pencil mark on the edges of a joker. The mark is made at the lower left and upper right edge, Figure 34. If the edge-marked card is placed into the deck, the mark will be visible as shown in Figure 35. The deck can be used for other tricks. When ready to perform "Conceal and Reveal," give the deck a shuffle or cut so as to bring the edge-marked card to the center. It need not be at the exact center of the deck, but try to get it as close as possible.

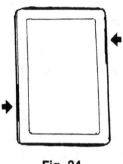

Fig. 34   Fig. 35

To present the trick, ask a spectator to lift off about half the deck, look at the face card of the cut portion, and replace this portion on top of the other packet. When he has done this, have him give the deck several straight cuts to further obscure the location of his card. Place the deck on the table so that you can see one of the long edges. Check whether the edge-marked card is near the center. If it is, do nothing. Otherwise, give the deck a cut so that the edge-marked card is shifted to a position close to the middle, and say, "I was going to try to find your card, but today I feel lucky." Turn to another spectator. "Ma'am, I'd like you to help us out also. Please cut off about half the deck and look at the card you cut to."

When she has done this, she replaces the cut packet back on top of the remainder of the deck. Then she gives the deck one or two straight cuts to randomize the position of her card. Place the deck on the table so that a long side is visible. Cut the deck and complete the cut as you tell the audience that now your task is twice as hard because you have to find two cards instead of one. Check the position of the edge-marked card. If it is not in the middle of the deck, give the deck one more cut to bring it to the middle.

Say, "I've never done this before, but I feel really lucky today. Let's have yet another person in on this. Sir, I'd like you to pick a card also." A third person cuts off about half the deck, looks at the face card of the packet he cut to, and replaces this packet on top of the remainder of the deck. He follows this by giving the deck one or two straight cuts. Take the deck. For the last time, check the long side of the deck to spot the position of the edge-marked card. If it is not in the middle of the deck, give the deck a cut to put the edge-marked card in the middle.

"I've never attempted to find three cards chosen by three different people. Let's make it really hard." Turn the deck face up and place it on the table. Cut off the face-most third of the deck and place it to the left. Cut off half the remainder of the deck and place it to the right. This packet is the key packet because, unknown to the audience, it contains all three of the chosen cards.

Spread each packet face up on the table and say, "We're doing everything in threes, so let's continue that way. I'd like each of you to remove a card from this packet [point to the packet on the left], this packet [point to the packet in the middle], and this packet [point to the packet on the right]. Just make sure that one of the cards you take is your selected card." Each spectator will take three cards, one from each group. Pay no attention to the cards taken from the left group or the center group. Remember each card taken from the right group.

Ask each spectator to mix his three cards. Take the three cards from one spectator. Pretend to have trouble, take one of the cards, shake your head, replace it, take another, replace that. Mix the three cards, then remove the one that the spectator took from the rightmost group. Place it face down on the table. Put the other cards aside face down. Repeat with each of the other groups of three cards. Have each party name their chosen card. Turn up your three choices to reveal a perfect score.

Sometimes one might want to perform this trick with a borrowed deck, but there is no opportunity to edge-mark a card. If the deck shows signs of wear, there is a simple way to edge-mark a card that was invented by Carmen D'Amico. After performing another trick, say a trick with the aces, hold the deck in the left hand. Insert an ace into

Fig. 36

the deck, but at an angle to the left. As the right fingertips push the card diagonally into the deck, the edge of the card slides past the nail of the left thumb, Figure 36.

The thumbnail scrapes against the card, leaving a streak or white line on the edge of the card. Practice to make sure that the nail engages the edge of the card for just a fraction of a second, only enough time to leave a short line. Square the card into the deck. Look at the left long side and the line will be clearly visible. This method puts a line on only one edge of the card. When doing the trick, make sure the deck is placed on the table so that the proper long edge is toward you. The working of the trick is otherwise the same.

MIND READING

Science has made great strides over the millennia, putting forth concepts and achievements unthinkable to our early ancestors. Much may have changed over the centuries, but belief in mind reading and the occult remain untouched by the march of science. The tricks in this chapter allow you to demonstrate diverse forms of mental magic. They all use borrowed cards.

29. Voodoo Clue

The effect is a prediction with a borrowed deck. It uses an offbeat application of a principle invented by Stewart James. If you plan to perform a series of mind reading tricks with a borrowed deck of cards, this trick is a good one to open with. The end result seems entirely out of your hands, yet the outcome is infallible.

The magician remarks, "Practitioners of voodoo and other forms of sorcery will pick up clues from the world around them. They practice with simple objects like playing cards." Spread the cards face up from left to right on the table, and secretly note the top card of the deck. We will say this card is the ♦A. Openly slide any 8-spot and any 9-spot out of the deck. Close up the spread and turn the deck face down. Say, "Before we begin, I'll explain that these two cards will serve as the influence cards. We will also need clue cards."

Push over the top seventeen cards without disturbing their order and without calling attention to the exact number of cards in use. Place this packet in front of the spectator. Put the balance of the deck in your pocket. Unknown to the audience, the top card of the seventeen-card packet is the ♦A. Invite the spectator to deal two equal heaps from the seventeen-card packet. He deals from left to right in the usual way, alternating a card to each heap. Explain that he can deal as many cards as he likes as long as the heaps are equal, and as long as there are some cards left over.

Let's say he deals two heaps of five cards each. The number does not matter, but make sure you know which heap contains the first dealt card, the ♦A. When he is through dealing, pick up the other heap, the one that does not contain the ♦A. Fan the cards so the audience can see the faces. "These are the clue cards. They tell us something about the future." Pretend to study these cards. Nod your head and put the packet in your pocket. On a piece of paper write, "ACE OF DIAMONDS." The card you write is always the card that was originally on top of the deck. Fold the paper, place it in plain view and say, "That is my interpretation of the clues."

Pick up the packet that contains the ♦A and place it on top of the remaining cards in the spectator's hand. Tap the two cards you placed aside at the beginning of the trick and say, "These are the influence cards. I chose an eight-spot and a nine-spot because they seemed the strongest of the many possibilities in the deck. Indicate one of these two cards." The spectator might choose the 8-spot. Direct him to transfer eight cards one at a time from the top to the bottom of his packet. The other card is the 9-spot. Direct him to transfer nine cards one at a time from the top to the bottom of his packet.

"We've seen the influence exerted by these two cards. Now let us find out if it achieved the proper convergence." Have the spectator turn the packet face up. The face card will be the ♦A. Ask someone to open the prediction. It correctly predicts that the ♦A will be chosen.

30. Magnetic Force

Magnetism is based on the principle that opposites attract. Magnetic cards operate on a contrary principle, the idea that like seeks like. From any shuffled deck, two cards are removed and placed face up on the table. Another card is chosen and magnetized by placing it in contact with the two face-up cards. The face-up cards might be a red seven and a black ten. The magnetic card succeeds in finding the other red seven and the other black ten. The trick is done with a borrowed deck. There is no prior preparation.

Method: With the faces of the cards toward you, spread the deck from left to right between the hands. As you do, secretly note the card that lies second from the top of the deck and the card that lies fourth from the top. Let's say these are a red seven and a black ten. Find the other red seven and the other black ten. Remove these two cards and place them face up on the table. Close up the deck and hold it face down in the left hand. Then tap each of the face-up cards and say, "These are our target cards, a red seven and a black ten. Let's see if we can succeed in finding cards like these."

Push over the top two cards of the deck as a unit. Take them with the right hand. Place them on the table without disturbing their order. Remark that magnetism exists in playing cards just as it does in the earth's magnetic field. One card indicates north, another card south. By handling the cards in pairs, the magnetic force is neutralized. Deal the next pair, and the next, and the next, and so on, placing each pair on top of the common heap. After you have dealt five or six pairs, ask the spectator to call "stop" at any time.

When he calls "stop," there will be a dealt packet on the table. The rest of the deck is in the left hand. Remove the top card of the dealt packet and turn it face up. "This will serve as our magnetic card. By separating it from the other cards, we can induce a new magnetic charge into the card." Rub the face-up card against the red seven and the black ten. Then drop it face up on top of the packet in the left hand.

Pick up the dealt packet and place it on top of the left-hand packet. The face-up magnet card is now buried in the deck. Again, deal pairs of cards off the top of the deck, placing them into a common heap on the table. When you have dealt past the face-up magnet card, ask the spectator to call "stop" at any time.

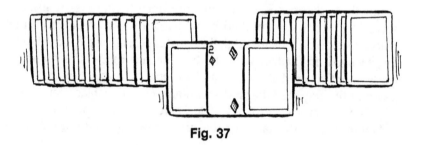

Fig. 37

Put the balance of the deck to one side and spread the dealt cards. Remove the magnet card and the card on either side of it, Figure 37. Turn these two cards over. One will be a red seven and the other a black ten.

31. Business Card ESP

People are likely to keep business cards if pleasant memories are associated with them. A useful and easy way for a magician to advertise is to use his business card in a magic trick. The business card is then given away as a souvenir to the spectator. This trick, a variation of a John Scarne effect, uses an ordinary deck of cards and two business cards. If business cards are not available, two slips of paper may be substituted. It is necessary to secretly glimpse the bottom card of the deck. This can be done after the deck has been given a cut or two. After glimpsing the card, I will usually give the deck one additional shuffle and cut, but of a special kind that keeps the bottom card in place. It is a simple sequence that is done as follows.

Assume the card you glimpsed on the bottom of the deck is the ♣A. Place the deck face down on the table, lift off the top half with the right hand, Figure 38, and place it to the right on the table. Both hands grasp their respective packets from above. The left thumb allows the bottom few cards of its packet to remain on the table. The two halves are then shuffled together, Figure 39, and squared up. The shuffle is followed by a cut. The right hand grasps the center twenty or so cards, pulls this packet out, Figure 40, and slaps it on top of the remainder of the deck. The deck has been given a fair shuffle and cut, but the bottom card (♣A) has been retained in place.

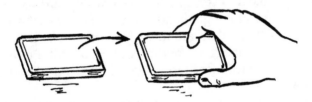

Fig. 38

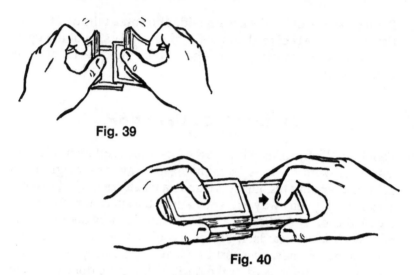

Fig. 39

Fig. 40

On the blank side of your business card write, "John will choose the ace of clubs." The person named in your prediction is one of the spectators who will participate in the trick. Place the business card on the table so the writing-side is down. Pick up the deck and place it face down in the left hand. Spread the cards from left to right between the hands. Ask John to touch a card in the top half of the deck. When he has done this, separate the hands so that the touched card is the top card of the left-hand packet.

Push this card to the right with the left thumb. An important part of the method takes place at this point. It is well covered and it is over in a second, but there should be no hesitation when it occurs. The right hand turns palm down and takes the touched card, Figure 41. But in the process, you must secretly glimpse the face card of the right-hand packet. In Figure 41, this card is the ♦7. As you take the card, say, "Let's see which card you picked as a marker." Turn the right hand palm up, Figure 42. "Ah, the five of hearts. We'll use that card to mark the place you chose." Leave the ♥5 in the outjogged condition of Figure 42. Place the left-hand packet face down on top of the right-hand packet, Figure 43.

"I feel lucky today. Mary, I'd like to try the same experiment with you." Put the deck face down on the table, and pick up another business card. On the blank side write, "DIAMONDS ARE

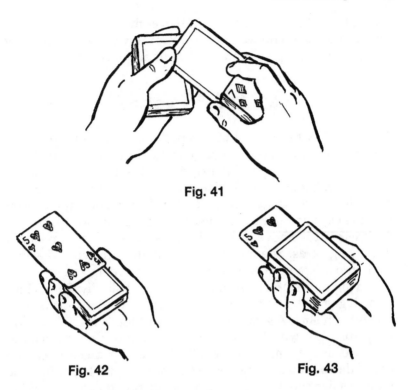

Fig. 41

Fig. 42   **Fig. 43**

FOREVER AND MARY WILL CHOOSE THE SEVEN OF DIAMONDS." Here
you write the name of the card you just glimpsed. Place the business card writing-side down on the table.

Pick up the deck and place it in the left hand. You are back to
the starting point, except that the ♥5 is in an outjogged condition
in the deck. Repeat the selection process for Mary. That is, spread
the cards and invite her to touch a card in the top half. Break the
deck at that point. The left thumb pushes over the touched card.
The right hand turns palm down and grasps this card (Figure 41).
The right hand turns palm up (Figure 42), and the left-hand
packet is placed on top of the right-hand packet (Figure 43).

Put the deck on the table, and spread the cards from left to
right. Take care to leave the face-up cards outjogged. Remove
each outjogged card and the card to the right of it (in other
words, the card that is face-to-face with each of the outjogged
cards). Next say, "Let's see how well we did. John, you stopped
me at—" Turn over the card that is paired with the ♥5 and

continue, "—the ace of clubs." Turn over the appropriate prediction to show that you were correct. Repeat with Mary's card. Let the spectators keep your business cards as souvenirs.

32. Cupid's Hotline

The effect in which a card trick is performed over the telephone was invented by John Northern Hilliard. This is a different version. On a slip of paper the magician writes down the business phone number of a professional psychic. On the back of the paper he jots down her home number. This is done in the event that the psychic can't be reached at the office number. A spectator is asked to remove four cards of the same value from a deck of playing cards. She might remove the four queens. They are dealt into a face-up row on the table in any order.

Playing card suits can be interpreted symbolically. Thus, clubs mean a golf club or a country club, in other words, something to do with athletics. A spade is another word for "shovel," symbolizing someone who is a builder. Hearts are of course linked to romance, and diamonds to wealth. The lady is asked to choose one of the four queens that represents her wish for the future. She indicates her choice by placing a coin or ring on any one of the four queens. The psychic is called. Without asking a single question, the psychic gives an accurate reading of the lady's wishes, and goes on to reveal the chosen card.

Method: There are actually two psychics, one we'll call psychic "A" and one we'll call psychic "B." A's phone number is printed on one side of the paper. B's number is the one you jot down on the other side of the paper. The audience doesn't know which is which, and assumes that either of these numbers will allow you to call the same person. But you can call either number the first time, and either number the second time. This gives you the four combinations necessary to code any one of the chosen cards.

The spectator chooses any four of a kind and deals them in a row in any order. Explain what the playing card suits symbolize. Let her choose a suit which represents her wish for current or future fulfillment. She does this by placing a small object on the appropriate card. It is best to use some object that has personal meaning to her, a ring, a bracelet, a watch or keys. Once she has made her choice, you then simply note the position of the card in the row, i.e., whether it is first, second, third, or fourth in the row.

Both of the psychics know you plan to call that evening. They should also know the approximate time you plan to perform the trick so they can be sure to be near the telephone. The first call that is made to the psychic is never answered. It is always necessary to make the second call, and that is the key to the mystery. We will go through one example to show how the system works. Let us say that the lady places a finger ring on the ♥Q. Instruct her to call A's number. Psychic A, hearing her phone ring, knows that she is the first to be called. She lets the phone ring until it stops.

Immediately she calls psychic B, lets the phone ring *once*, and hangs up. This informs psychic B that the first call was to A. That first call tells both psychics that the chosen card was red. At his end, the magician says, "Hmm, no answer. She should be there. Maybe she stepped outside for a moment. Try the number again." The lady calls A's number a second time. Psychic A already knows that the chosen card is red. If psychic A is called both times, the chosen card must be the ♥Q.

If the spectator chose the ♦Q, psychic A is called first. She does not answer the phone. When the phone stops ringing, she calls psychic B to tell her she got the first call. When the magician asks the spectator to try again, he instructs her to call the second number. Psychic B knows that the card is red. The fact that she gets the phone call tells her that the chosen card is the ♦Q.

Here is another example. Say the lady places the finger ring on the ♣Q. Instruct her to call B's phone number. Psychic B, hearing her phone ring, knows that she is the first to be called. She lets the phone ring until it stops. Then she calls psychic A, lets the phone ring once and hangs up. This informs psychic A that the first call was to B. Both psychics know that the chosen card was black. At his end, the magician says, "Hmm, no answer. Maybe she stepped out for a moment. Let's try the other number. We might have better luck." The spectator calls A's number. Psychic A knows that she was not called the first time, but she was called the second time. The chosen card is black. The second phone call tells her the chosen card is the ♣Q.

In sum, if psychic A gets the second phone call but not the first, the chosen card is the ♣Q. If she gets both phone calls, the chosen card is the ♥Q. If psychic B gets the second phone call but not the first, the chosen card is the ♦Q. If she gets both phone calls, the chosen card is the ♠Q.

33. Contemplation

A magician need not have complete knowledge of a chosen card in order to bring the trick to a successful conclusion. In this trick, the magician has secret knowledge of only one thing, the suit of a card merely thought of by a spectator. By means of a simple procedure, he is able to reveal the identity of the thought card.

Method: When the borrowed deck is handed to you, hold it so you can see the faces. Spread the cards from left to right. Beginning at the rightmost part of the deck, upjog the first diamond you come to. Now upjog the first club you come to after that, then the first heart you come to after that, then the first spade you come to after that. Thus far the situation looks like Figure 44.

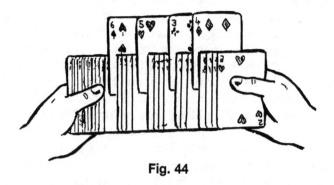

Fig. 44

Continue to spread the cards from left to right. As you do, repeat the above procedure by upjogging the first diamond you get to, then the first club, then the first heart, then the first spade. There are eight upjogged cards at this point. Upjog one more set of four cards in the same suit order. Finally, upjog a single card. This is the thirteenth card that has been upjogged, and it should be a joker.

The above procedure insures that you will have an equal distribution of suits. Square up the deck side-for-side. Strip the thirteen upjogged cards out of the deck. Hold the thirteen cards in the left hand and place the rest of the deck aside. The packet of thirteen cards is face up so it is easy to glimpse and remember the face card of the packet. Say this card is the ♦A. Turn the packet face down.

You want to mix the cards to give the illusion that you don't know what any of the cards are. At the same time, you want to position the ♦A so that it is sixth from the top of the packet. The handling is as follows. Holding the packet face down in the left hand, push the top two cards to the right. Grasp them from above with the right hand, Figure 45, and drop them onto the table. Push over the next two cards, grasp them from above with the right hand, and drop them onto the tabled cards. Push over the next pair of cards and drop them onto the tabled cards. Push over a single card, take it from above with the right hand, and drop it onto the tabled cards. Finally, drop the balance of the packet on top of all. Done casually, it looks as if you gave the packet a series of quick cuts. The important point is that the ♦A has been secretly positioned sixth from the top of the packet.

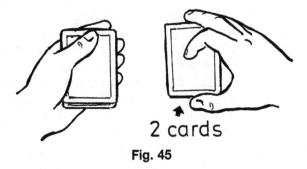

2 cards

Fig. 45

Hand the packet to the spectator and turn your head aside. Ask him to fan the cards so he can see the faces. Invite him to think of any card in the packet. He then closes up the packet. Next, instruct him to spell the color of the card by dealing a card at a time into a tabled heap, one card for each letter. "For example, if you are thinking of a red card, you would spell R-E-D, and deal a card for each letter into a tabled heap. Deal the cards silently so I don't know what you are doing." After the spectator has done the spell–deal procedure, he drops the remainder of the packet on top of the dealt heap.

Now ask him to think of the value of the thought card. "If you are thinking of an ace, for example, you would spell A-C-E and deal a card for each letter into a heap on the table." After the spectator has performed the spell–deal procedure for the card's value, he drops the remainder of the packet on top of the dealt heap. Say, "Finally, I'd like you to think of the suit of the card you are thinking of. If it is a club, you would spell C-L-U-B-S, dealing a card for each letter." After the spectator has performed the spell–deal procedure for suit, he drops the remainder of the packet on top of all.

Take back the packet. Look for the ♦A. If it is now fifth from the top of the packet, the thought-of card was a heart. If it is third from the top, the thought card is a diamond. If the ♦A is seventh from the top, the thought card is a spade. If it is eighth from the top, the thought card is a club.

Let us say the ♦A is seventh from the top. There are three spades in the packet. He could have chosen any one of these three cards. You want to narrow down the possibilities to one card. It is done by asking two questions. The questions will vary depending on the three cards you are dealing with, but the strategy is always the same. In general terms, you want to find differences among the three cards. One may be a high card, one may be an odd-value card, one may be a picture card.

Let's say the spectator's three cards are the ♠4, ♠8 and ♠J. Here is how you narrow down the choices. "There are several picture cards in this packet. Is your card a picture card?" If the spectator says yes, he picked the ♠J. Remove this card from the packet and place it face down on the table. Ask him to reveal the identity of his thought card. When he does, turn over the card on the table to reveal that you correctly tuned in to his thoughts.

If he says he is not thinking of a picture card, you know the card must be either the ♠4 or ♠8. Both are even-value cards, but one is relatively high in value, one relatively low. Say, "You aren't thinking of a picture card, but is it a card with a value higher than seven?" If he says yes, it must be the ♠8. Otherwise, it is the ♠4.

Remove the appropriate card from the packet and place it face down on the table. Ask the spectator to name the card he was thinking of. Turn over the tabled card to reveal that you were correct.

Your advantage in this trick is your secret knowledge of the suit of the spectator's card. The audience thinks you are faced with the challenge of finding one out of thirteen cards, but it is really a choice of one out of three. When asking the spectator to think of a card, request that he not think of the joker as you plan to use the joker to focus your thoughts.

34. Opposite Twins

There is a saying that everyone has an opposite twin. The truth of that proposition is demonstrated in this impromptu mental test. Remove the ♥A through ♥5 and arrange them in numerical order from the top down. Remove the ♠A through ♠5 and arrange them in numerical order. Place one packet on top of the other. These ten cards are all you need for an offbeat three-part routine.

Hand the packet to a spectator and turn your head to one side. Direct him to place the packet behind his back. Once it is out of sight, ask him to give the packet several straight cuts. He is then to take either the top or bottom card and hide it in his pocket. The rest of the packet is handed over to you. "They say that opposites attract. You chose a card and hid it in your pocket. It could be either red or black. I'm going to try to find a card of the opposite color that matches your card."

Grasp the packet by the ends from above with the right hand, while the left thumb slides the top card off. Simultaneously, the left fingers slide the bottom card off the packet. This action is that of the Klondyke shuffle shown in Figure 13, page 22. The left hand places this pair of cards on the table. In similar fashion, draw off the next pair and place it onto the tabled cards. Repeat with each of the next two pairs. There will be a single card remaining in the right hand. Give this card to the spectator and have him drop it into his pocket.

Pick up the eight-card packet. Hold it face down in the left hand. Push over the top four cards. Flip them over all at once and drop them face up onto the remaining cards. It is important that the order of these four cards be maintained when they are flipped over. Say, "Now we're going to try something more difficult. Some cards are face up, some face down. I'm going to ask this lady to choose a card. If she picks a face-up card, I'm going to endeavor to pick the opposite, a face-down card, that will match the value of her card."

Turn your head to one side. Hand the packet to the lady. Ask her to give the packet several straight cuts, and then to remove either the top card or the bottom card and place it on the table. She is then to cover this card with the card case. Take the balance of the packet from her. Remove pairs of cards as you did before, drawing one off the top and one off the bottom each time, as in Figure 13, and placing them into a tabled heap, until you have one card left. Your card will be either face up or face down. Assume it's face up. "My card is face up. If opposite twins do indeed exist, this means that your card is face down. Is that true?" The lady will say yes. Slide your card under the card case.

"Now comes the hardest test of all. I'm going to remove pairs of cards from those that remain, but I will be guided only by my sense of touch." Pick up the packet of six cards and place them behind your back. Withdraw the top and bottom card as in Figure 13. One card will be face up and one face down. Place this pair of cards on the table, then repeat with each of the other pairs.

"Let's see if opposite twins do exist." Ask the first spectator to withdraw the two cards from his pocket. They will have matching values. Lift the card case from the next two cards. One of these cards is face up and one face down. Turn the face-down card over to reveal that it matches the value of the other card. There are three pairs of cards on the table. Turn up the face-down card of each pair to show a perfect match.

35. Mental Mate

Anyone picks up his own pack and gives it a thorough shuffle. Then he splits the deck approximately in half, turns one half face up and shuffles the two halves together several times. All shuffling and cutting is honest and outside the magician's control.

The spectator is asked to think of a number between 1 and 20.

He is asked to deal cards off the top of the deck into the performer's hand and to silently count to the thought-of number, but he is to count face-down cards only and ignore the face-up cards that come off the top of the deck. The magician turns his head away as the cards are dealt into his hand. When the spectator reaches the thought number, he calls "stop," looks at the last card dealt and places it on top of the deck.

The packet counted off the top of the deck is then squared and returned to the top of the deck. The spectator writes the name of his card on a piece of paper and pockets the paper for the moment. The magician says that he too will think of a number, but to avoid thinking of the same number as the spectator, he asks the spectator to tell the audience his thought-of number. Let's say the spectator's number is 7.

The magician says that his number is 17. Taking the deck, he deals cards into the spectator's hand, counting face-down cards only, and stopping when he gets to the seventeenth face-down card. He looks at this card. The deck is then assembled and shuffled. The magician writes the name of his card on a piece of paper. When his card is compared with the spectator's, it is found that the magician chose the ♥5 while the spectator chose the ♦5. In other words, each party chose the mate of the other person's card.

There are no key cards and no preparation. The deck need not be complete. The magician sees only one card, the card he himself chose, yet he always ends up with the mate of the spectator's card.

Method: Instruct the spectator to cut off about half the deck, turn it face up and shuffle it into the other half. Ask him to think of a number between 1 and 20. Turn your head to one side. Ask him to deal cards off the top of the deck into your hand. He is to count only face-down cards, and he is to continue the count until he reaches his chosen number. While he does this, keep silent count of the *total* number of cards dealt into your hand, up to and including the spectator's final card, the one corresponding to his thought-of number. Let's say the total number of dealt cards is twenty-four.

Tell him to look at this last card and replace it on top of the deck (not on top of the packet in your hand). He is to write the name of his card on a piece of paper. As he does so, turn over the packet in hand. Then drop it on top of the deck to bury the spectator's card. To avoid picking the same number, have the spectator tell the audience his thought-of number. In telling them his number, he is also telling you. We will say his thought-of number is 7. Subtract it from your number, 24, add one, and announce to the audience that your number is 18.

Next, take the deck from the spectator. Deal cards into his hand off the top of the deck. Count aloud the number of face-down cards you deal until you reach your thought-of number. The audience thinks you have gone far beyond the spectator's chosen card, but in fact the eighteenth card *is* his card. Look at it and place it face down on top of the packet in your hand. Take the dealt packet from the spectator's hand and place it on top of all to bury your card.

Place the deck on the table. Pick up a piece of paper and a pen. Do not write the name of the card you just saw. Instead write down the name of the mate of this card, in other words, the card of the same value and same color but opposite suit. If the spectator's card is the ♦5, your card will be the ♥5. All that remains is to have your writing compared with the spectator's. As impossible as it may seem to the audience, you and the spectator have chosen the mate of one another's card.

36. Greeks Bearing Gifts

A tale is told of the Dorian who was captured by the ancient Greeks. When the Greek ruler learned that his captive was a magician, he asked him to perform a few tricks, promising him his freedom in exchange. The Dorian explained that his specialty was cards, whereupon the king replied that since playing cards hadn't yet been invented, the magician would have to use the pictures of four prominent oracles.

At this point, the magician removes the four queens from the deck, has them initialed, and asks that they be thoroughly mixed by a spectator. A card is chosen from the packet of queens, returned and the packet again shuffled by the spectator. Taking the cards, the magician looks them over and promptly removes the chosen queen.

On witnessing this, the king remarked that the trick was a good one. However, he said, "Three queens remain, so entertain us with a trick using just those three cards."

The three queens are placed in a face-down row on the table. While the magician turns his back, the spectator places a coin on the back of one of the queens. He places the other two queens in his jacket pockets, one on each side. The magician turns and faces the audience. After a moment of concentration, he names the card on the table, the one covered with the coin.

"An excellent trick," the king observed, "but two queens still remain. Now do a trick for us with those two cards."

These two queens are concealed in the spectator's jacket pockets, one on either side. While the magician turns his back, the spectator removes one of the cards and hands it to the magician behind his back. After a great effort at concentration, the magician names the card without looking at it.

"Superb!" exclaimed the king. "Now if you can perform a trick with the remaining card, I will be satisfied."

The magician replies, "That trick was accomplished before I came here today." So saying, he removes a sealed envelope from his pocket and hands it to a nearby spectator. The spectator opens the envelope, removes a piece of paper, unfolds the paper and reads, "The last queen will be the queen of clubs." The prediction is correct.

Method: On a piece of paper write, "THE LAST QUEEN WILL BE THE QUEEN OF HEARTS." Fold this paper, seal it in an envelope, and place it in your right trouser pocket. On another piece of paper write, "The last queen will be the queen of diamonds." Fold this paper, seal it in an envelope, and place this envelope in your right jacket pocket. It is easy to remember that the *red* suits are on the *right*. Similarly, place a ♣Q prediction envelope in your left trouser pocket, and a ♠Q prediction envelope in your left jacket pocket. This is the only preparation, and it is done before you plan to perform this trick.

Because you will have someone write his initials on the faces of the cards, it is wise to use your own cards. When ready to do the trick, remove the four queens from the deck and have someone initial the upper right corner of the face of each queen. Gather the queens so the initials are all at the top right. Turn the packet face down and mix the cards. Fan the cards, Figure 46, and invite a spectator to remove one card and remember it. Close the fan by placing your forefinger at the upper left corner of the fan, Figure 47. Swing the cards around

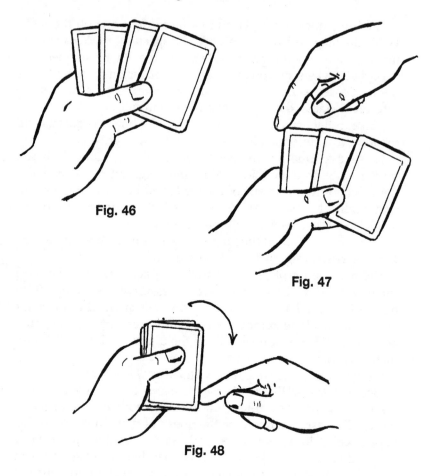

Fig. 46

Fig. 47

Fig. 48

as shown by the arrow in Figure 48. This has the effect of reversing them end-for-end.

Ask the spectator to insert his card into the packet. Hand him the packet and have him mix the cards. When he is satisfied that the cards are well mixed, take back the packet. Fan it so you alone can see the faces. The initials on one queen will be opposite to the others. Remove this queen and place it face down on the table. As you look for the chosen queen, memorize the suit order of the other three queens. This sets up the next two tricks.

Tap the tabled queen. Ask the spectator to reveal the identity of his chosen card. When he does, turn over the tabled queen to show that you correctly found his card.

Deal the remaining three cards in a row on the table. Turn your back. Ask the spectator to place a coin or other small object on any queen. There are two queens remaining. He is to place his left hand on the leftmost of these two cards, and place this card in his left jacket pocket. Then he is to place his right hand on the other card, and place this card in his right jacket pocket. Turn and face the audience. There is a card on the table with a coin on top of it. This card is still in its original position. You memorized the order of the three cards, so as soon as you see the position of the card, you know its identity. Pretend to concentrate. Then reveal the identity of this card.

For the third effect, turn your back once again. Ask the spectator to remove either card from his pocket and hold onto it for a moment. Say, "Have you done that?" As you speak, turn slightly so you can see which hand he used to remove a card. Once again, because you memorized the order of the three queens, you know which queen is in which pocket. For this reason, you now know the identity of the card he holds in his hand. Face away from the audience. Ask the spectator to give you the card behind your back. Pretend to mull things over. Then reveal the name of this card.

Turn and face the audience. You are required to perform a trick with the remaining queen. Reach into the proper pocket, remove the prediction envelope, and have the prediction read aloud. Once again you are correct.

NOVELTY TRICKS

In an earlier era, card magic could be divided roughly down the middle. On one side were those tricks dependent on sleights like the two-handed pass and the classic palm. On the other were those that relied on counting and dealing to achieve the desired outcome. Magicians starting out were thus faced with narrow and restricted choices; if they did not want to spend hours learning difficult sleights, they had to settle for dealing tricks too simple to be called magical.

In the twentieth century, magicians formulated ideas that replaced sleights and counting with subtlety and smooth handling. Modern-day magicians now enjoy options undreamed of in an earlier era. The tricks in this chapter exploit some of these new avenues.

37. Back Stop

To the classic stop trick has been added a comedy angle that produces an amusing and surprising result. The spectator chooses any card. It is buried in the deck. Even the magician doesn't know the location of the chosen card. The magician deals cards off the top. Unexpectedly a card shows up that has the word "STOP!" printed on it.

The "stop" card is turned over. Printed on the back are the words, "BACK UP 3 CARDS." The magician does, and the card he turns up is the chosen card.

Method: Because of the unexpected ending, this is a good trick to use as an opening trick. It signals that your magic is different from the usual run of things.

It is necessary to secure a playing card that is blank on both sides. These are available at stores that sell supplies to magicians. Another method is to find a thin cardboard that has the same

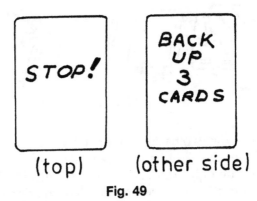

(top)   (other side)

Fig. 49

consistency as a playing card. Blank postcards are a good choice. Cut a piece that is the size of a playing card. The blank card is filled out as shown in Figure 49. Once made, it can be used over and over. Position the "stop" card third from the top of the deck.

The means used to control the chosen card in a fair-seeming manner was invented by Tony Bartolotta. It is easy to do and creates the appearance of a chosen card hopelessly lost in the deck. Start with the deck in the left hand. Grasp it from above by the right hand. Release cards off the bottom of the deck as shown in Figure 50. For most people it is easier to release cards off the thumb than the fingertips. Strive to release them in a steady stream rather than in bunches.

Ask the spectator to call "stop" as you release cards. When he does, lift the portion of the deck that is still in the right hand. Ask him to remember the face card of the right-hand packet. Lower the right-hand packet, and place it on the table to the right of the other heap. Grasp each heap from above. Cut the top half of the left-hand packet to the left. Simultaneously, cut the top half of the right-hand packet to the right. The action of the cut is shown in Figure 51. Complete the cut of each packet.

Fig. 50

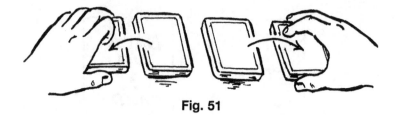

Fig. 51

There are now two packets on the table. The chosen card is in the middle of the right-hand packet. Pick up this packet from above with the right hand. At the same time, lift off half of the left-hand packet with the left hand. Place the right-hand packet between the two groups of cards on the left as shown in Figure 52. Square up the deck, cut the top third of the deck to the table and complete the cut.

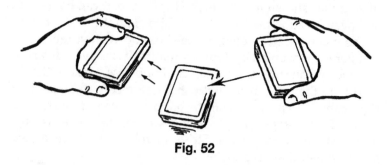

Fig. 52

The above description suggests that a lengthy process is involved, but it takes just seconds to complete. Because both hands move simultaneously, it does not seem that a secret control can be accomplished. The audience does not know that the chosen card is three above the "stop" card.

Remark that you are going to try a very difficult trick. You are going to deal the cards as fast as possible, yet you will stop at the precise location of the chosen card with complete accuracy. After you make this statement, add, in a less assured voice, "In the rare event that I overshoot the mark, there is an insurance policy that kicks in automatically." Next, deal cards off the top of the deck into a heap on the table. Deal as fast as you can, first because that is part of your claim, but more importantly because it allows you to get to the surprise finish without too much delay.

When you get to the "stop" card, deal it onto the tabled heap. "That's the insurance card I was talking about." Turn it over onto the heap. The writing on the reverse side says, "BACK UP 3 CARDS." Lift off the "stop" card, and place it on the table for the count of one. Lift off the next card for the count of two, and place it on the table. Lift off the next card for the count of three, and place it on the table. Ask the spectator to name the chosen card. When he does, lift off the next card and turn it over. It will be the chosen card.

38. Suspense

Magicians make a distinction between a levitation and a suspension. In a levitation, an object or a person rises into the air. When this is done with playing cards, it is called a rising card effect. In a suspension, the object or person remains suspended motionless in midair with no visible means of support. While the suspension effect is not often done with playing cards, this is one such example. A deck of cards is stood upright, and the card case is stood upright near it. A playing card is placed on top of both. The card case is removed, yet the playing card remains suspended as shown in Figure 53. The suspended card may be tossed to the audience. The deck can be used for further card magic.

Method: An inconspicuous gimmick makes the trick work. The gimmick is a piece of transparent tape about one inch in length. Fold up the bottom third, Figure 54, and fasten it to the middle third. This leaves about a third of the sticky surface exposed, as shown by the shaded portion in Figure 55.

Fasten the tape to the back of the ♦3 as shown in Figure 56. The prepared card can be carried in the pocket until you are ready to

Fig. 53

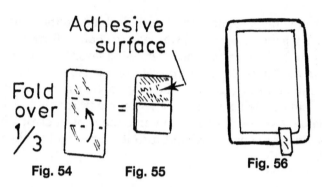

Fig. 54   Fig. 55   Fig. 56

perform the trick. Drop the deck into the pocket, then bring it out again with the ♦3 on the bottom. Make sure the tape extends from the deck at the inner end, and that it is concealed from audience view by the left hand, Figure 57. With the right hand, withdraw a few cards from the back of the deck and transfer them to the face. This puts the ♦3 a few cards in from the face of the deck.

With the exposed tape at the bottom and therefore concealed by the left hand, spread the cards from left to right until you reach the ♦3. Upjog this card for about half its length. Next, close the deck side-for-side. Angle the ♦3 out of the deck so that only a corner (the gimmicked corner) is still in the deck, Figure 58. Place

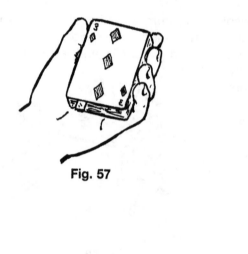

Fig. 57

Fig. 58

the deck in an upright position on the table. It is held in this vertical position by the left hand. Instruct the spectator to place the upright card case about two and a quarter inches away from the deck. He is to hold the card case upright.

Your left hand holds the upright deck. Your right hand slides the ♦3 up to *just* the point where it clears the top of the deck. The tab is still in the deck. Hinge or rotate the ♦3 down, so it rests on top of the deck and the card case, Figure 59. Note in Figure 59 that the left forefinger curls in against the deck and pushes against the face of the deck. At the same time, the thumb and other fingers pull back. These opposing forces keep the cards tightly in place, and prevent the tab from slipping out of the deck.

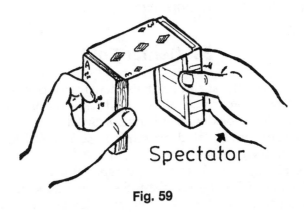

Spectator

Fig. 59

Pretend to hypnotize the card. Then have the spectator slowly slide the card case away. The ♦3 remains mysteriously suspended as shown above in Figure 53. It is an odd sight. All that is required now is to get rid of the gimmick. The right fingers contact the face of the ♦3, and the right thumb the back. The card is hinged forward, i.e., it is pivoted up so that the face of the ♦3 will be visible to the spectator, Figure 60. The left hand maintains firm pressure on the deck. The result is that the ♦3 is peeled away from the tape, leaving the tape in the deck with the sticky surface protruding from the top of the deck.

While the right hand moves the ♦3 to the position shown in Figure 60, the left forefinger changes position and presses down on the tape as is also indicated in Figure 60. The forefinger

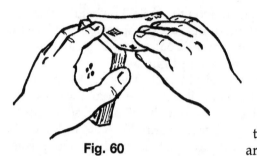

Fig. 60

completely covers the tape from audience view. Shake the ♦3 with the right hand as you patter about removing the spell. In the meantime, the left forefinger slides around to the far long side of the deck. As it does so, it takes the tape with it since the tape is now stuck to the forefinger. The left hand releases the deck, while the right hand tosses the ♦3 to the spectator. The palm-down left hand then drops to the lap and rolls the tape off the forefinger.

39. Center Fold

The occasional offbeat and unconventional card trick is a change of pace from more classic plots. This trick is an offbeat double prediction. It can be done with any borrowed deck, but because a card will be torn in half during the course of the trick, it is best to use your own cards.

A joker is signed on both sides by a spectator so it can be identified later on. The magician places the joker and the deck behind his back, and inserts the joker into an unknown location in the deck. Now two cards are chosen. The cards are freely selected and are not known to the magician. One card is returned to the deck face down, and the other card face up. "There are two selected cards, but only one joker." To remedy the situation, the magician makes a tearing motion with the deck. Then he cuts the deck in half.

Half of the signed joker is found next to the first selection. The other selected card is face up. Addressing the second spectator, the magician says, "Your card is face up, so let's tap the cards to turn the other half of the joker face up. Then we'll tap the card again to put the joker next to your card." When the cards are examined, it is seen that the face-up half-joker is indeed adjacent to the face-up chosen card.

Method: It is a good idea to carry a joker with you. That is all you need to perform this trick with any cards, even a borrowed deck. The back design and color of the joker need not match those of the deck.

Have the joker signed front and back. As this is done, explain that you don't want anyone to suspect that you switch jokers, and the signature front and back keeps things honest. Hold the face-down deck in one hand, the joker in the other. Explain that you are going to place the joker into the deck at a location that is unknown even to you. Put both hands behind the back. When the cards are out of sight, perform the following actions.

With the cards out of sight, silently tear the joker across the middle down to the midpoint of this card. Then wrap the joker around the side of the deck as shown in Figure 61. Place the deck in left-hand dealing position. Bring the deck into view, the face of the deck toward the audience. The joker is concealed from audience view because the left fingers cover the wrap-around condition of the joker.

Riffle along the upper-right corner with the right forefinger until the spectator calls "stop," Figure 62. The right forefinger moves into the break. The right thumb and forefinger then slide the top portion above the break to the right, and clear of the deck. Figure 63 shows the start of this action.

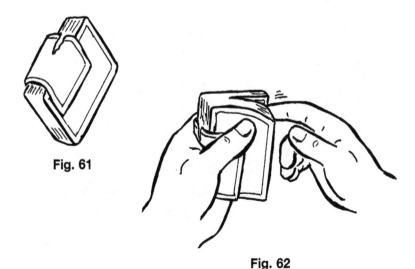

Fig. 61

Fig. 62

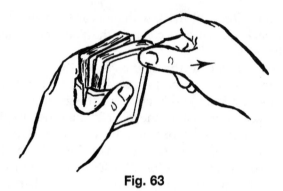

Fig. 63

Have the first spectator note the face card of the portion held in the right hand. This portion is placed on top of the balance of the deck. With the hands removed for clarity, the situation at this point is shown in Figure 64.

Again, the right forefinger riffles along the outer-right corner of the deck until "stop" is called by a second spectator. Time it so that "stop" is called when the forefinger is in the top quarter of the deck. Lift off these cards with the right hand in the same way as is shown above in Figure 63. Have the second spectator shuffle these cards, note the top card, and turn it face up on top of the packet. Take this packet with the right hand, and place it under the packet held in the left hand, Figure 65.

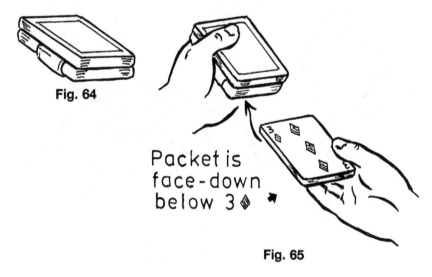

Fig. 64

Packet is
face-down
below 3♦

Fig. 65

With the aid of the right hand, lift or pivot the deck to a vertical position. The back of the deck faces the left palm. Break open the deck at the midpoint as if opening a book, Figure 66. Grasp one-half of the deck in each hand, Figure 67. Hold each half firmly. Remark, "Two cards have been chosen, but I have only one joker. To remedy the situation, I should tear the joker in half." Make a tearing motion, the left hand moving down with its packet, the right hand moving up with its cards. This will tear the joker in half.

Place the right-hand packet on the table. Turn the left-hand packet face down. Spread the cards slowly between the hands. When you get to the half-joker, comment on the fact that it is face down. Slide it and the card above it out of the spread. Turn the card over to reveal the first chosen card and say, "The face-down portion of the joker found a face-down card. Now we need the other half of the joker to find a face-up card." Tap the other half of the deck. "That turns the joker face up." Tap the packet again. "And that puts it right next to your card." Spread through the cards until you get to the half-joker. It will be face up, and it will be just above the second selected card.

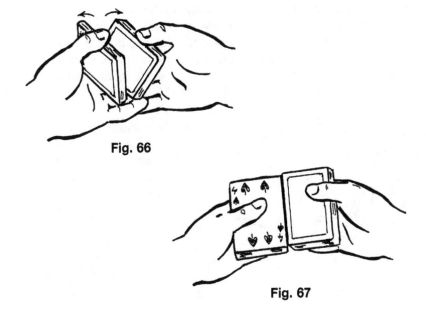

Fig. 66

Fig. 67

40. Krazy Kut

Gamblers practice ways to follow the cards through shuffles and cuts. That way they know where certain cards are during the game, and can shape their strategy accordingly. One such system works as follows.

The magician glances through a borrowed deck. Then he gives the deck two cuts. "A card I saw, the four of clubs, should now be tenth from the top of the deck." The magician counts to the tenth card and it is the ♣4. He gives the deck two more cuts. "This time I cut a little deeper. Another card I saw, the nine of diamonds, should now be eleventh from the top." He counts to the eleventh card. It is the ♦9. One more time he gives the deck two quick cuts. "This time I cut deeper still. The queen of clubs should be exactly twelfth from the top." He counts to the twelfth card. It is the ♣Q.

The trick contains a bonus feature that we shall describe after we explain how the trick is done.

Method: The trick is really a swindle. When the borrowed deck is handed to you, glance through it and remember the cards that lie tenth, eleventh, and twelfth from the top. The rest of the demonstration is a matter of handling a fake cut.

Talk to the audience about the way gamblers follow the track of certain cards through shuffles and cuts. Hold the face-down deck in the left hand, and grasp the deck from above with the right hand, Figure 68. The left hand takes the lower half of the deck, turns palm down, and deposits this packet on the table, Figure 69.

The left hand then turns palm up, takes the remaining packet from the right hand, turns palm down, and places this half of the deck on top of the tabled half, but in the offset condition shown in Figure 70. The left hand remains in a palm-down position as it grasps the entire deck, turns palm up, and brings the deck

Fig. 68

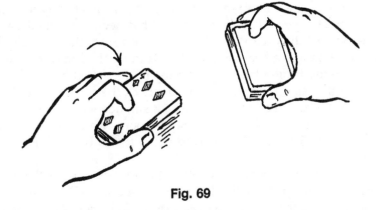

Fig. 69

up to the right hand, Figure 71. The right hand lifts off the upper packet and places it on the table. Then the right hand takes the remainder of the deck and places it squarely onto the tabled portion. This completes the double cut. It appears to the audience as if the deck has been fairly cut each time. Actually, the deck is back in its original order.

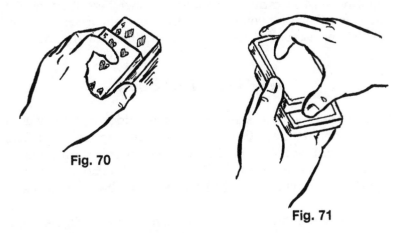

Fig. 70

Fig. 71

Name the card that was tenth from the top, the ♣4. Count ten cards into a heap on the table. Turn up the last card dealt and it will be the ♣4. Turn this card face down onto the tabled heap. Pick up the tabled heap, and place it back on top of the deck. Repeat the double cut exactly as described above. The only difference in the patter is your statement that this time you will cut a little deeper. After the double cut has been performed, say, "The nine of diamonds should be eleventh from the top." Deal eleven cards into a heap on the table. Turn up the last card dealt. It will be the ♦9. Replace the ♦9 on top of the tabled heap.

Place the tabled heap on top of the deck. Perform the double cut once more and say, "This time I cut still deeper. The queen of clubs is exactly twelfth from the top." Count twelve cards into a tabled heap. Turn up the last card dealt. It will be the queen of clubs.

With all of the cutting and dealing, the audience thinks that the deck is mixed up. Actually, the cuts were self-cancelling, and the dealing only affected the top twelve cards. This means that if you are using your own deck and require a partial setup for a trick, you can put the stacked cards near the bottom of the deck. Cut off the top half of the deck and hand it to the spectator for shuffling. Take back the shuffled cards, glance through them, and memorize the tenth, eleventh, and twelfth cards. Put this portion back on the balance of the deck and perform "Krazy Kut." Then cut the stack to the top, and you are ready to perform the trick requiring stacked cards. The audience remembers shuffling the cards, and they saw you give the deck several cuts. As a result, they will never suspect a stack is used in the follow-up trick.

41. Seen, Not Seen

In most prediction tricks the prediction is hidden from view until the last minute. Paul Curry suggested an opposite approach, where the content of prediction is known from the beginning. His trick bears the apt title, "The Open Prediction." This is a repeat version which may be done with any borrowed deck of cards.

After looking through the top ten cards of the deck, the magician writes on a piece of paper, "MIKE WILL SELECT THE ACE OF SPADES." The prediction is placed in full view so that all may read it. Mike is asked to think of a number from 1 to 10. He tells no one his number. He is asked to deal cards one at a time off the top of the deck into a face-up heap on the table. When he gets to the thought-of number, he is to deal that card face down.

No one knows when he will deal a face-down card until the moment he does so. Let's say that he deals the seventh card face down.

"The ace of spades has not shown up so far," the magician says. "That is a favorable omen. I'm inclined to try it again with the same lucky number. Since I know the number, it would be unfair of me to look at the faces of the cards. All I'd have to do is look at the seventh card. This time, I'll look at the cards from the back and base my prediction on that."

On a new piece of paper he writes, "MIKE WILL SELECT THE THREE OF DIAMONDS." Mike deals cards into a face-up heap. When he gets to the seventh card, he deals it face down. The ♦3 hasn't shown up yet. "Of course, the ace and the three could be further down in the deck, but that would be cheating. The ace and the three are right here." The two cards Mike stopped at are turned face up. One is the ♠A and the other is the ♦3.

Method: Besides the deck of cards, you will use a couple of pieces of paper and a marking pen. Something will be used to hold the two chosen cards. A drinking glass is ideal. The card box can also be used. When the deck is handed to you, ask the spectator to think of a number between 1 and 10. Pretend to think things over. Remark that you will look through the first ten cards to see if you can guess which card he is going to pick. Actually, you ignore the first ten cards and concentrate on the eleventh card. Say this card is the ♠A. Close up the deck and hand it to the spectator.

On a piece of paper write in bold letters, "MIKE WILL PICK THE ACE OF SPADES." The use of a marking pen guarantees that the writing can be clearly seen by all those in attendance. Leave the prediction on the table. Ask Mike to deal cards off the top of the deck one at a time into a face-up heap. When he gets to his thought-of number, he leaves that card face-down. The deal stops as soon as he has dealt the face-down card.

Of course, he will not have seen the ♠A. Remark that this is a favorable omen. Take the face-down card and place it into the glass, the back of the card to the audience, Figure 72. As you do, glimpse the identity of this card. Let's say it is the ♦3. There is a pile of face-up cards on the table. These are the cards dealt off the top by Mike. Gather them, turn them face down, and drop the deck on top of these cards.

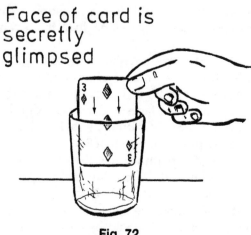

Face of card is
secretly
glimpsed

Fig. 72

"Maybe Mike's chosen number is a lucky number. I'm going to test it again, but this time without looking at the faces of the cards." Pick up the deck and deal cards one at a time into a face-down heap until you have dealt ten cards. Stare at the cards as if getting psychic vibrations. Act as if you have received a particularly strong signal. On a fresh piece of paper write, "MIKE'S SEC-OND CARD WILL BE THE THREE OF DIAMONDS." The name of the card you write on the paper is the card that is already in the glass.

Place the dealt packet on top of the deck. Ask Mike to deal cards off the top one at a time. As before, when he gets to the thought-of number (in this case 7), he is to deal that card face down. After he has dealt a card face down, he can continue to deal several more cards face up just to see if the ♦3 turns up.

Take the face-down chosen card and drop it into the glass. Gather all the face-up cards, turn them face down, and put them back on top of the deck. Remove the two prediction cards from the glass. Hold them face down in the left hand. Take the top card with the right hand and slip it under the packet. Take the new top card and slip it under the packet. Do this four or five more times as you say, "The vibrations are strong and positive. Now, the moment of truth." Look at the faces of the cards. Remove the ♠A (the first card you predicted) and toss it face up onto the ♠A prediction. Turn the ♦3 face up and toss it onto the ♦3 prediction for a perfect score.

42. Faces and Aces

Art Altman invented a card trick where face-up and face-down cards acted in a mysterious manner. This is a simplified handling. A twist has been added to further surprise the audience.

A spectator removes four random cards from the deck. He chooses one of these and turns it face up. His chosen card plus the remaining three cards are shuffled back into the deck. He alone knows the identity of his chosen card. The deck is then spread face up on the table. The spectator's four cards have somehow reversed themselves in the deck. These four cards are removed. The magician correctly identifies the spectator's card and tosses it out face up. For the unexpected finish, the other three cards are then turned over. They have changed to aces.

Method: Before the start of the trick, remove the four aces from the deck and place them in your shirt pocket. You may perform other tricks with the remainder of the deck. When you are ready to perform "Faces and Aces," have the spectator shuffle the deck and take half the cards. Take the remainder of the deck with your right hand and say, "Please shuffle your cards and deal the top four cards in a row on the table." After the spectator has dealt four cards into a face-down row, take the balance of his packet and turn your back. "Please turn one card face up. Remember this card. Drop the other three cards face down on top of it."

With your back turned, reach into your shirt pocket and remove the four aces. Place them face up on your left palm. You are holding the deck in your right hand. Drop the deck face down on top of the aces. Finally, withdraw the bottom ace and take it in your right hand. Assume that this is the ♠A. Turn and face the spectator. "I've taken an ace from my cards. We'll use it in a minute." Toss the ♠A face up to the table, and drop the deck face down on top of the spectator's packet. If you were to examine the pack at this point, you would have a large group of face-down cards, then three face-up aces, then three face-down cards, then the spectator's face-up chosen card.

Pick up the deck, place it face down into the left hand and say, "You picked four cards, so we will turn the deck over four times." Turn the deck over end-for-end. Then turn it over side-for-side. Then turn it over end-for-end, and finally turn it over side-for-side. Say, "We cut the deck three times," as you lift off the top third of the deck and place it on the table. Lift off half of the remainder and place it onto the tabled portion. Put the remaining third of the deck on top of all.

"We shuffle the deck twice." Turn the deck face up. Cut off half and place it alongside the other half. Riffle shuffle the two halves together. Try to make it as even a shuffle as possible. After the shuffle, cut the top half off and shuffle it into the other half. The deck is now face up on the table. "And we tap the deck once." Pick up the ♠A and tap it against the face card of the deck. Put the ace aside.

"After four turnovers, three cuts, two shuffles and one tap, an odd thing happens." Spread the deck face up on the table. The entire deck is face up except for four cards. "Your four cards have reversed themselves." Slide the four reversed cards out of the deck. Fan them so you alone can see the faces. Remove the card that is not an ace and hold it in the right hand. "What card did you choose?" When the spectator names his card, turn over the card in the right hand to show that you correctly picked out the chosen card. This appears to be the end of the trick, but you have one more surprise to spring on the audience.

"It was easy finding your card. I know it wasn't this ace." As you say "this ace," tap the ♠A. "Or this ace, or this ace, or this ace." As you say these words, toss each of the other aces face up on the table.

THE DECK IS STACKED

When only a few cards need to be set up, the cards can be arranged while the performer is toying with the deck. Since some tricks make use of a more extensive stack, the cards must be arranged beforehand. You don't want the audience to suspect that the cards are stacked, so it is advisable to perform several tricks with a duplicate deck, drop the deck into the pocket, then pretend to remember there was one more trick you wanted to do, and remove the stacked deck. Here are three tricks that make use of stacked decks.

43. Would I Lie?

Most politicians do admirable work running the government, but sometimes people doubt whether campaign speeches are entirely loyal to the truth. In this trick, the spectator's ability to separate truth from a politician's tall tales is tested.

The deck is cut into three heaps. Playing the part of the politician, the magician notes a card from the middle heap and jots it down on a piece of paper. Let's say the card is the ♦A. He makes several statements of a political nature. Spectators are asked to decide if he is lying or telling the truth. If they think he is lying, they take the top card of a packet that is labeled, "ALL LIES." If they think he is telling the truth, they take the top card of a packet labeled, "THE TRUTH." The process continues until the spectators have a total of four cards.

To measure their ability to size up a politician, they add together the values of the four cards, and count that many cards in the deck. They arrive at the card chosen by the magician, the ♦A.

Method: Cut out two pieces of paper, each the size of a playing card. On one, in bold letters write, "THE TRUTH." On the other write, "ALL LIES." Next, turn to the deck, where a few cards need to be stacked. Arrange to have any ace on top, followed by a 4, 2, and 6. At positions 38-39-40-41 have any 7, 3, 5, 2. The stack is shown in Figure 73.

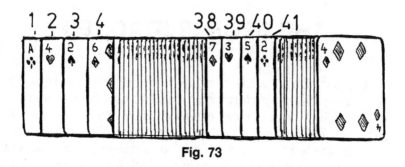

Fig. 73

Separate the deck at the ♦7 and turn each packet face down. The top card of one packet is the ♣A. The top card of the other packet is the ♦7. Place the two pieces of paper on top of the ♦7 packet. Then place the ♣A packet on top of all, Figure 74.

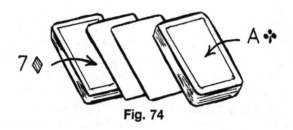

Fig. 74

Finally, it is necessary to know ahead of time the card you are going to choose. Look at and remember the card that lies seventeenth from the top of the deck. Let's say this card is the ♦A. Place the deck in the card case until the time of performance. This trick should be performed as a comedy card trick. People suspect politicians of stretching the truth when they run for office. You can work local political issues into the patter to increase audience interest. For the purpose of this trick, we will use more general questions of a political nature.

Remove the deck from the card case and place the cards on the table. Lift off the packet above the two pieces of paper. Put this large packet on the table alongside the smaller bottom portion of the deck. Remove the two pieces of paper and show them. Leave the papers on the table, writing side up. Invite the spectator to lift off about half the cards from the larger packet and place this portion to the left. This is packet A in Figure 75. The top card of this portion is the ♣A. Next to this heap put the paper that says "THE TRUTH." The small packet labeled packet C in Figure 75 is the original bottom portion of the deck. It has the ♦7 on top. Next to this heap put the paper that says "ALL LIES."

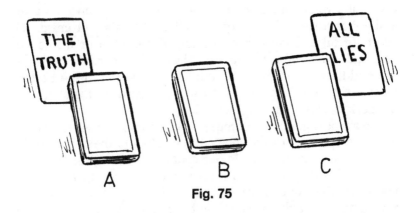

Fig. 75

You are now ready to perform the trick. "We know that some politicians will say anything to get elected. I'm going to play the part of Senator Poobah. He's running for reelection this year and he's been heard making some interesting statements. Let's see if you can size up the senator. Our control element will be a card that I'll choose." Lift up a portion of the cards in the center packet (B). Pretend to note the card you cut to, and replace the cut portion. On a piece of paper, write down the name of the card you noted earlier, the ♦A.

"If you think the senator is telling the truth, take the top card of this group." Tap the top card of packet A as you say this. "If you think the senator is telling a lie (or, as he would put it, a highly unlikely truth), take the top card of this group." Tap the top card of packet C as you say this. The first statement the spectator is asked to evaluate might be, "If elected, I will almost certainly double the salary of every gainfully employed person in this great state of ours." The spectator takes either the top card of packet A or the top card of packet C.

The second statement might be, "If elected, I will eliminate the tolls on all our toll roads and provide free cheeseburgers at rest stops." Again the spectator takes the top card of packet A or packet C. The third statement might be, "When elected, I pledge I will not take taxpayer-paid vacations to Hawaii unless absolutely necessary." In response to this statement, the spectator takes the top card of packet A or the top card of packet C.

The fourth statement is the one all politicians make at some time in their careers. "I promise I will absolutely never raise your taxes, unless, of course, an extreme national emergency requires a slight increase." In response to this campaign promise, the spectator takes a card from the top of packet A or the top of packet C. Reassemble the deck by placing the top packet (A) onto the middle packet, and this combined packet onto the bottom packet (C). Except for the four cards removed by the spectator, the deck is back in its original order.

You are now going to test the spectator's ability to separate truth from lies. Ask him to add together the values of the four cards he picked. The total might be 14. He counts to the fourteenth card in the deck. It will be the ♦A. Turn over the piece of paper on which you wrote the name of the card you picked. It says you chose the ♦A. Congratulate the spectator on his political acumen.

44. After Dark

The spectator plays the part of the wizard by correctly guessing a card chosen by the magician. At the same time, the magician correctly guesses a card chosen by the spectator. The magician is the one who actually figures out the identity of each card. There are many ways to accomplish this, but we will use the simplest method, a full deck stack. The stack in question is known as the "Eight Kings" stack. The deck is arranged as follows from the top down:

♣8-♥K-♠3-♦10-♣2-♥7-♠9-♦5-♣Q-♥4-♠A-♦6-♣J
♥8-♠K-♦3-♣10-♥2-♠7-♦9-♣5-♥Q-♠4-♦A-♣6-♥J
♠8-♦K-♣3-♥10-♠2-♦7-♣9-♥5-♠Q-♦4-♣A-♥6-♠J
♦8-♣K-♥3-♠10-♦2-♣7-♥9-♠5-♦Q-♣4-♥A-♠6-♦J

As a check on the stack, the ♣8 will be the top card of the deck, the ♥8 will be fourteenth from the top, the ♠8 twenty-seventh from the top, and the ♦8 fortieth from the top. The bottom card of the deck will be the ♦J.

The title of the stack gets its name from the mnemonic device used to remember the stack, which is, "Eight kings threatened to save ninety-five queens for one sick knave." (When this particular mnemonic device was invented, a jack was known as a "knave.") The meaning of it is, "Eight kings three-ten to seven nine five queen four ace six jack." Go over the mnemonic device a few times until you commit it to memory. Then test yourself as follows. After the deck has been stacked as described above, cut the deck and complete the cut. Look at the bottom card. Whatever its value, recite the mnemonic device until you get to that value. The next value in it is the value of the top card of the deck, which means that by knowing the bottom card, you also know the top card.

The suits are arranged in clubs-hearts-spades-diamonds order. The first letter of each suit spells "CHSD." This is easy to remember if you picture the word "CHaSeD." If the deck is given a complete cut and the top card is a club, the next card must be a heart, the next a spade, and so on.

To perform "After Dark," arrange the deck in the Eight Kings setup beforehand. At the time of performance place the deck on the table and give it several straight cuts. Say, "We're going to try something a little different. I'm going to pick a card first." Remove the top card of the deck, look at and replace it on top of the deck. There is no need to remember this card. You are only making a pretense of choosing a card.

Give the deck two or three straight cuts to place your card at a random location. Slide the deck toward the spectator and invite her to give the deck several straight cuts. When she stops, remove the top card, place it to one side sight unseen and say, "This card you cut to might have special meaning later on." Now have her look at the new top card of the deck. She then replaces this card on top and gives the deck several straight cuts.

Take the deck from her. "Let's see if I can correctly locate your card." Spread the cards between your hands. The colors will alternate red-black-red-black from top to bottom, but there will be one point where two cards of the same color are side by side.

This is because one card was removed and placed aside. Assume the two same-color cards are red. Cut the deck between them and complete the cut. Look at the bottom card. Whatever it is, move one ahead in the mnemonic device, and you will arrive at the identity of the card placed aside. For example, if the bottom card is the ♦6, the card placed aside will be the ♣J. You will then pretend that you chose the ♣J.

Place the deck face down on the table. Remove the top card and place it face down on the table. "Let's see if we are on the same wavelength. What card did you choose?" The spectator will name the ♥8. Turn over your card to show you correctly guessed her card. "My card was the jack of clubs. I didn't see it in the deck. Do you suppose that the card you cut to . . ." Let your voice trail off as you point to the card placed aside earlier. Turn it over to reveal the ♣J.

45. Psi-X

Some tricks seem to offer no clue as to how they might be done. In this trick, the magician hands the deck to a spectator and turns his head to one side so he can't see any card. The spectator cuts off a portion of the cards, gives it a shuffle, and places it on the table. He then looks at the top card of the balance of the deck and places this card on top of the shuffled portion. Finally, the spectator shuffles the balance of the deck and drops it on top of the chosen card. The deck is squared and handed to the magician. The magician looks through the deck, narrows his choice to five cards, then three, then one. This card is removed from the deck and placed face down on the table. The spectator names his card. He then turns over the tabled card to reveal that the magician found the chosen card.

There are no gimmicks. The deck is ordinary. No questions are asked. The spectator has a free choice. The chosen card is buried somewhere in a deck shuffled by the spectator. The magician has no idea what the card is, nor where it is located in the deck, yet he invariably finds the correct card.

Method: The deck is stacked before the trick begins. The stack is simple and easy to remember, yet it is the key to the working of this mystery. Stack the diamonds in numerical order from ace to king. Place this packet face down on the table. Stack the spades in numerical order and place them on top of the diamonds. Stack the hearts in numerical order and place them on top of the spades. Finally, stack the clubs in numerical order and place them on top of all. The ♣A is the top card of the deck and the ♦K the bottom card. This trick should be done as an opening trick. Otherwise, you can perform a trick that does not disturb the stack.

When ready to perform "Psi-X," place the deck face down on the table. Turn your head to one side and invite the spectator to cut off a portion of any size from the top of the deck. Direct him to give this packet a thorough shuffle. He then places this packet face down on the table. Ask him to look at and remember the top card of the balance of the deck. He places this card on top of the shuffled portion. Then he picks up the remainder of the deck, gives this packet a good shuffle, and drops it on top of all. The chosen card is buried between two shuffled packets. No one knows its location in the deck.

Pick up the deck. Spread the cards so you alone can see the faces. Beginning with the face card, silently say, "Ace of clubs." Push over the second card and silently say, "Two of clubs." Continue in this way, reciting the names of the cards from ace to kings of clubs, then ace to king of hearts, and so on. Most of the way, the card you push over to the right does not correspond to the card in your mental recitation. But somewhere along the way, you will silently say the name of a card that corresponds to the card you have silently pushed over. The card that matches the card in your mental checklist is the chosen card. Upjog this card about an inch. Upjog four more cards further along in the deck.

Remark that you have it narrowed down to five cards, and ask the spectator to concentrate on his card. Push one of the upjogged cards square with the deck, then another and another and another, until just one card (the chosen card) remains. Remove this card and place it face down on the table. "Tell us the card you picked." When the spectator names his card, direct him to turn over the tabled card. It will be his card.

Every once in a while the spectator will shuffle the cards in such a way that one card in the shuffled packet is still in its original position. It happens rarely, but to cover yourself for this possibility, when you find a card that matches your mental count, don't stop. Continue the mental checklist through to the end of the deck. If you find two matches, say the ♦5 and ♣3, narrow it down by saying, "Was your card a red card?" If the spectator says yes, you know he chose the ♦5. If he says no, reply, "I thought not." Either way you know the chosen card and can go on with the revelation as described above.

RED-BACKED BLUES

When red-backed and blue-backed cards are used together, the combination adds color and novelty to the performance. Such cards may be found anywhere that playing cards are sold.

46. One Second Flat

Opening tricks give the audience a chance to get to know the magician. Such tricks work especially well when they combine humor and surprise. In "One Second Flat," the magician pretends to expose the secrets of the professional gambler. The secrets are mostly jokes, but there is a surprise double ending.

You will use a red-backed deck and a blue-backed joker. Remove the ♦A-♦K-♦Q-♦J-♦10 from the red-backed deck. Arrange them so they are second, fourth, sixth, eighth, and tenth from the top of the deck. Turn the deck so it is face up and place it on the table. Drop a blue-backed joker on top, Figure 76. The preparation is complete. Case the deck in the card case belonging to the blue-backed deck.

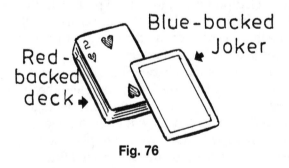

Fig. 76

When ready to perform this trick, comment on the fact that a lot of gambling secrets are easy to learn. In fact, you claim, you can teach them to anyone in one second flat. Take the cased deck from the pocket. Remove it so that the blue-backed joker shows. The appearance is that a blue-backed deck is being removed from a blue card case. Toss the case to one side, and place the deck on the table so the blue-backed card is on top. "Here, I'll show you. Because of the ingenious construction of this ordinary seeming deck, I can cut to any card and identify that card in one second flat."

Place the right hand on top of the deck and grasp the deck by the ends. Lift off the top half and place it in the left hand. The first joke is revealed: the deck is really face up. Tap the top card of the tabled heap, Figure 77, and say, "That card is the three of clubs [or whatever card you cut to]."

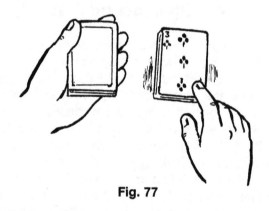

Fig. 77

Place the tabled portion on top of the portion in the left hand. "I can tell you are impressed. Here's another use for this gambler's deck. I'll name a card, let's say the joker. With this special deck, I can find the joker in one second flat."

Spread the deck quickly between the hands until you get to the face-down card. Cut the deck and complete the cut so that the face-down card is on top. Flip it over to show that it is the joker. Turn the joker face up and show it to the audience. They see that it has all been a gag and are willing to play along. But here you turn the tables a bit to set up the unexpected finish. Slide the face-up joker under the face-up deck. By a bit of trickery, you are about to reinforce the impression that the entire deck is blue-backed. It is done as follows.

Lift off about ten cards with the right hand, Figure 78. Place this packet face up on the table. Turn the left hand palm down,

Figure 79, as you point to the face card of the tabled packet and say, "The genius who invented this deck came up with the idea to mark the faces rather than the backs. This card, for example, is the four of diamonds." Turn the left hand palm up again. Cut off another ten or so cards with the right hand, Figure 78. Place this packet on the tabled group of cards. Turn the left hand palm down as you point to the new face card of the tabled group. "And this card is the eight of clubs."

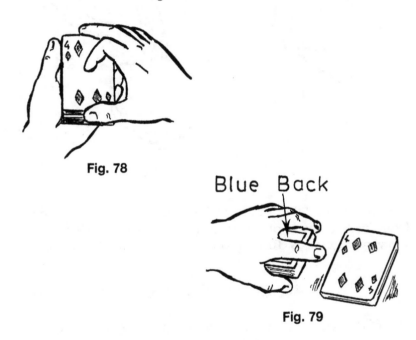

Fig. 78

Blue Back

Fig. 79

Turn the left hand palm up again. Cut off another group and place it onto the tabled cards. Turn the left hand palm down, point to the face card of the tabled packet and say, "And this is the king of clubs." Turn the left hand palm up again. Place the tabled cards onto the cards in the left hand. The face-up deck has been assembled. The point to be made here is that in Figure 79 the audience sees the back of a blue-backed card. Since this is done three times, it subliminally reinforces the idea that the entire deck is blue-backed.

Slide the joker out, flash the back and drop it in the pocket. Say, "Gamblers switch decks too. They can do it in one second flat."

Hold the deck as shown in Figure 80. Turn the left hand palm down and immediately draw the deck out of the left hand with the right thumb and fingers, Figure 81. Spread the deck between the hands to show that the deck is now red-backed.

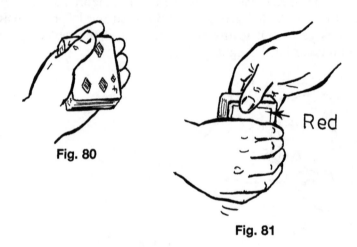

Fig. 80

Red

Fig. 81

Next say, "And they can stack the deck in one second flat too." Deal out two hands of poker. Turn up the spectator's hand to show average cards. Turn up your hand to show a Royal Flush.

47. Colors Can't Mix

One of the basic assumptions about magic tricks is that they will be brought to a successful conclusion. Sometimes a trick is puzzling because it doesn't work. This is one example. The magician removes four black cards from a blue-backed deck and four red cards from a red-backed deck. With the cards face up, he mixes the colors. But when the cards are turned face down, the backs have refused to mix. The magician then mixes the face-down cards so that blue-backed and red-backed cards are mixed. When the cards are turned face up, they have once again refused to mix. This is the author's routine for a premise suggested by Ron Edwards.

Method: Beforehand, remove the ♠3 and ♠4 from a blue-backed deck and the ♥A and ♥2 from a red-backed deck. Place these cards aside, as they will not be used in this routine. To complete the preparation, place the red-backed ♠3 and ♠4 into the blue-backed deck. Place the blue-backed ♥A and ♥2 into the red-backed deck. Case the decks and you are ready to begin.

When you are ready to perform the trick, remove the red-backed deck from its case. Spread the cards face up, explaining that you want to use a few red cards from this pack. Slide the ♦A out of the pack. Place the ♦2 on top of it, the ♥A on top of that, and the ♥2 on top of all. The remainder of the red-backed deck is gathered and placed aside. Remove the blue-backed deck from its case, and spread the deck face up on the table. Remove the ♣3 from the spread. Place the ♣4 on top of it, the ♠3 on top of that, and the ♠4 on top of all. The situation at this point is shown in Figure 82. Gather the blue-backed deck and place it to one side.

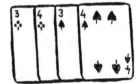

Fig. 82

Square the two packets and turn them face down. Drop the blue-backed packet on top of the red-backed packet. Immediately pick up the combined packet and spread it out face up. "In order for this trick to work, the colors have to be mixed. What I mean is that reds and blacks have to be mixed like this." Remove the ♣3 and place it on top of the ♥2. Insert the ♣4 between the ♥2 and ♥A. The ♠3 goes between the ♥A and the ♦2, and the ♠4 goes between the ♦2 and ♦A. The intermixed cards are shown in Figure 83. When you handle the cards, take care that the front end of the spread or fan of cards points slightly downward. This not only increases visibility (you want the audience to see exactly how the colors are being mixed), but it also guarantees that the backs of the cards won't accidentally be seen by the audience.

Square the packet, keeping the cards face up. Deal the four face cards into a heap on the table, reversing their order. Drop the remaining four cards on top of them and say, "Good. The faces of the cards are mixed, and that means that the backs are also

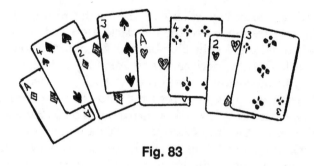

Fig. 83

mixed. We can proceed with the trick." Turn the packet face down in your hands and spread the cards. The backs have *not* mixed. Red-backed cards are on one side, blue-backed cards on the other.

You are ready to perform the second part of the trick. "Hmm. The backs refused to mix. Let's start over." Keep the cards face down. Spread them in a loose fan in the left hand, Figure 84. Place the card at the face or bottom of the spread, card A in the illustration, on top of the packet. Card B goes between H and G. Card C goes between G and F. Card D goes between F and E. The intermixed cards are shown in Figure 85.

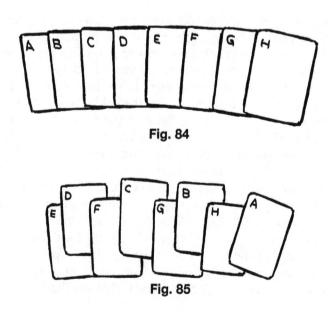

Fig. 84

Fig. 85

Place the top pair (A plus H) to the table. Place the next pair (B plus G) under the packet. Place the next pair (C plus F) onto the tabled cards. Drop the remaining four cards on top of all. The colors should be mixed, but when the cards are spread, it is seen that reds are on one side, blacks on the other. Remark that the colors must be jinxed and put the cards away.

48. A Volatile Card

The performer explains in advance that he has a prediction card in his pocket, and further, that it is from another deck. "The prediction has to be isolated because it has a habit of affecting everything it comes in contact with." A blue-backed deck is removed from its case and a card is chosen, say the ♥6. The ♥6 is placed face up on the table, and the prediction card is removed from the pocket. It is red-backed. When turned face up, it is seen to be a matching ♥6.

The performer accidentally cuts the red-backed ♥6 into the blue-backed deck. Realizing his mistake, the magician says, "I shouldn't have done that. Here's why." The deck is turned face down and spread across the table to show that it has become red-backed. As an added touch, when the prediction card is turned over, it is seen now to be blue-backed.

Method: Remove the ♥6 from a red-backed deck, put it into an envelope, and drop it into the pocket. Remove the ♥6 from a blue-backed deck and place it on top of a red-backed deck. Slide the deck into the blue card case.

To perform the trick, remove the deck from its case, but keep the deck face up. Close the flap on the case and place it on the table in front of you. Turn the deck face down and place it on top of the case crosswise, so it can later be picked up easily without fumbling. Remove the envelope from the pocket and say, "There's a card inside the envelope, but it has a volatile nature, so I have to keep it isolated from other cards." Drop the envelope on the table.

The palm-down left hand grasps the deck by the ends, turns palm up and allows the deck to fall into the left hand in the position shown in Figure 86. Explain to the spectator that you are going to remove groups of cards from the deck, and he is to call "stop" at any time. Lift off a packet of about eight or nine cards with the right hand and place them crosswise on top of the card box as shown in Figure 87. Continue transferring small packets from the deck to the card case until the spectator calls "stop."

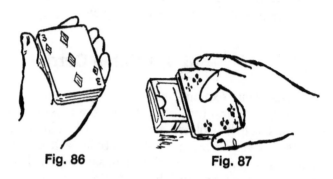

Fig. 86   **Fig. 87**

When "stop" has been called, take the balance of the deck from the left hand and place it crosswise on top of the cards that are on top of the card case. The back card of this packet is the blue-backed ♥6. The situation is shown in Figure 88. Pick up the envelope and slide the ♥6 out face down. Toss the envelope to one side. Do not show the audience the face of this card just yet.

Attention is now directed to the deck. Lift up the upper packet. Keep it face up. Slide out the back card of this packet and as you do this, say, "This is where you stopped me, at the six of hearts." Drop this card, still face up, onto the table. Replace the

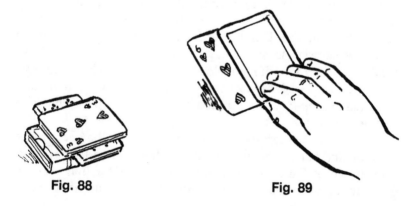

Fig. 88   **Fig. 89**

packet on top of the card case. Drop the red-backed card on top of the ♥6, but in an offset condition. "Let's see if the prediction is correct." Grasp the two cards as shown in Figure 89. Keeping them in the offset spread position, turn them over together. The audience sees that the prediction exactly matched the chosen card. This appears to be the point of the trick, but there is more to follow.

With the blue-backed card uppermost, square the two cards. Drop them onto the face-up deck. Cut the deck and complete the cut. Snap your fingers as if suddenly remembering that you shouldn't have done that. "I should never have allowed that red-backed card to come into contact with the deck."

Spread the deck face down on the table to reveal that the deck is now red-backed. "Look at that. The deck turned red . . ." Push the face-up ♥6 out of the deck as you say, ". . . and the prediction card turned blue!" Turn the face-up card over to reveal the blue back. Drop the blue-backed card into the envelope and pocket the envelope. You are left with a complete red-backed deck, and can now perform further mysteries.

49. Subliminal Force

"Throughout each day we are bombarded by advertising messages. Some function on a subliminal level. Here's a group of cards that are used to test subliminal forces. We can think of them as individual advertisements. They look pretty much the same, but one is different from the others. The difference will be obvious once it is pointed out, but otherwise it is invisible. I've recorded this unusual card on a piece of paper."

The test uses ten playing cards. The spectator is given a free choice of a card. A paper clip is attached to this card. The card looks like all the others, but when the difference is pointed out, it is indeed obvious and unmistakable. Needless to say, this card matches the writing on the piece of paper. The trick is based on a card effect suggested by Arthur Carter.

Method: Nine blue-backed cards and one red-backed card are used in this test. One of the blue-backed cards is red, say the ♦5. The other blue-backed cards are black spot cards. The red-backed card is the ♠3. Arrange the ten cards as shown in Figure 90. The

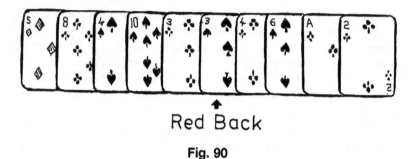

↑
Red Back

Fig. 90

blue-backed ♦5 is on top of the packet, and the red-backed ♠3 is sixth from the top.

On a piece of paper write, "YOU WILL CHOOSE THE ONLY RED CARD." Fold the paper. Place the cards and the paper into an envelope along with a paper clip. If you receive official-looking documents in the mail, put them into the envelope too. This creates the impression that they were mailed to you for the performance of this test. When ready to present the trick, remove all the contents of the envelope. Take care to keep the cards squared, so you do not reveal the presence of the red-faced card or the red-backed card.

Hold the packet face up in the left hand. With the aid of the left thumb, push over to the right the face-most five or six cards. Do not spread all the cards because you want to keep the ♦5 hidden from view. Remark that although the cards look pretty much the same, one card is different from the others. The difference is invisible until it is pointed out; then it becomes obvious and unmistakable.

Square the packet, still keeping it face up. Push off the five face-most cards without disturbing their order. Place this group of cards on the table. Turn the remaining five cards face down. Drop this group on top of the tabled cards. Pick up the packet with the right hand, grasping the packet by the ends. The Klondyke shuffle is going to be enacted. Draw the top and bottom card off together with the left thumb and fingers, Figure 13, p. 22. This pair of cards will consist of a face-down card on top of a face-up card. Drop this pair of cards on the table. As you do so, remark that you are going to mix the cards. Draw off the next top and bottom card the same way. Drop this pair on top of the tabled pair. Do the same with each of the remaining three pairs of cards.

Pick up the ten-card packet and hold it in the left hand. "We're going to use a random card to pick a card. Please give me any number from one to ten." It does not matter which number the spectator chooses. Say he names 4. Push off the top three cards, counting them aloud as you do so. Don't reverse the order of these cards, and place them on the table. Put the paper clip on the fourth card, and drop this card onto the tabled heap. Drop the remainder of the packet on top of all. Deal the ten cards into two rows as in Figure 91. Deal the first card to position 1, the next to position 2, and so on.

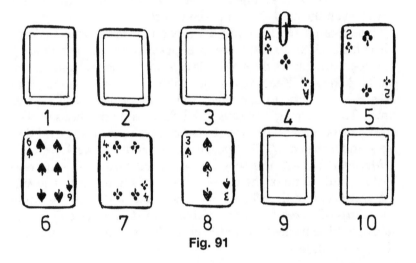

Fig. 91

Point to the paper-clipped card. "Wherever the paper-clipped card landed, we are going to use the card at the same position in the other row as our chosen card. No one could possibly know in advance that we would arrive at this card, yet a subliminal force must have been at work." In the example of Figure 91, you will use the card at position 9 as the chosen card.

The ending of the trick follows a simple rule. If the chosen card is face down, turn all of the other cards face up. If the chosen card is face up, turn all of the other cards face down. Do not turn over the chosen card during this process; turn over all of the *other* cards. Open the prediction. It says, "YOU WILL CHOOSE THE ONLY RED CARD." Point out that the prediction refers to the other side of the chosen card. Turn this card over. It will be either the only red-backed card or the only red-faced card.

50. Any Named Ace

"I was experimenting with card tricks using red-backed and blue-backed cards. Some of them were accidentally mixed together." A deck of cards is shown to consist of a mixture of red-backed and blue-backed cards. "Before I separate the colors, I thought it might be interesting to do a trick using some of these cards. This is the first time I'm going to try this trick. In fact, it's a trick even the cards haven't seen before."

Sixteen cards are dealt into array on the table. The magician turns his back and says, "Aces are lucky cards. Name any ace." The spectator names the ♦A. He is directed to place a coin on any red-backed card. Keeping his back to the audience, the magician asks the spectator to slide the coin from card to card several times. Then the magician says, "Which ace did you choose?" The spectator says it was the ace of diamonds. "Turn up the card that rests under the coin." The spectator does and it is the ♦A.

Method: You will use seven blue-backed cards and nine red-backed cards. One of the blue-backed cards is the ♣A. The ♠A, ♥A and ♦A are red-backed. All of the other cards are low-value spot cards of mixed suits. These sixteen cards are stacked. In this stack, B=blue-backed, R=red-backed. From the top down the stack is as follows:

♣A-B-R-B-♠A-♥A-R-B-♦A-B-R-B-R-B-B-R

Get eighteen more red-backed cards and eighteen more blue-backed cards. Shuffle them together and place the combined packet face down on the table. Drop the stacked packet on top of all. You now have a deck consisting of fifty-two cards of mixed back colors. Put the cards in the card case until the time of performance.

At the time of performance, remove the deck from the case. Spread the cards face down on the table to show the mixture of red-backed and blue-backed cards. Square the deck and turn it face up to show a random distribution of playing card values and suits. Square the deck and turn it face down. Deal the cards into four rows, dealing from left to right. Each row contains four cards. When you have dealt sixteen cards, the layout will look like Figure 92.

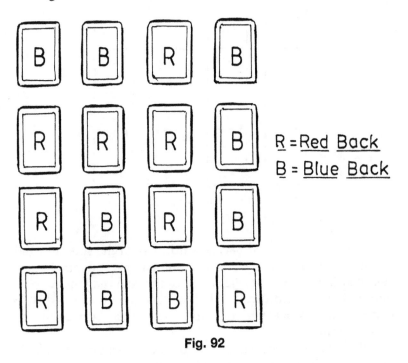

R = Red Back
B = Blue Back

Fig. 92

Unknown to the audience, the aces are distributed as shown in Figure 93.

Turn your back. Ask the spectator to name any ace. Then ask him to place a coin on any red-backed card. It does not matter which ace he chooses and it does not matter where the coin goes. The first four directions you give him are always the same and will always bring the coin to the same card. When he has placed the coin on a red-backed card, say, "We're going to move the coin around. I want this process to be strictly random, so I won't look. Please move the coin left or right to the nearest blue-backed card."

After he has done this, say, "Good. Please move the coin up or

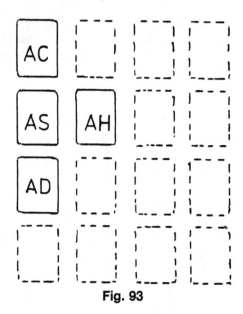

Fig. 93

down to the nearest red-backed card." When the spectator tells you he has done this, say, "I'm beginning to get a mental impression that the ace is near. Please move the coin diagonally to the nearest blue-backed card." When he has done this, say, "We're getting close. Move the coin up or down to the nearest red-backed card."

Unknown to the audience, the coin now rests on the ♠A. The instructions have been arranged to deliver the coin to the ♠A because this is the ace most people name. If the spectator chose the ♠A, the trick is over. Turn and face the spectator. Have the chosen ace named again. Then have the card under the coin turned over to reveal that it is the ♠A.

If the spectator picked any other ace, there is an additional move. The coin rests on the ♠A. If he named the ♣A, have him move the coin up one card. If he picked the ♥A, have him move the coin to the right one card. If he picked the ♦A, direct him to move the coin down one card. When doing the trick, remember to increase the excitement in your voice as the coin moves closer and closer to the correct ace on each round.

ROLL THE DICE

Dice have characteristics that are useful in the performance of magic tricks. In some tricks, dice are manipulated by sleight of hand. In others, the mathematical properties of dice are exploited. The tricks in this chapter make use of the fact that dice can be used to generate random numbers; keep rolling the dice and new numbers show up all the time.

51. Cast of Cards

When cards and dice are combined, the result is often an offbeat trick. In this routine, two packets of cards are placed before the spectator. He rolls a single die. We'll assume a 5 is rolled. He removes and discards any 5's that may be in one of the packets. Then he turns the die over. Now a 2 shows, so he removes any 2's that may be in the other packet.

The magician draws a line across the middle of the face of a joker. The spectator writes the number 5 above the line and the number 2 below the line. "This conveys a certain power to the joker, the power to attract other cards to it. Let's see if the power is working today." The joker is placed reversed between the two packets. The combined packet is then placed on top of the deck.

The spectator deals out five poker hands. One of the hands contains the reversed joker. The other hands are turned over one at a time. None of these hands contains a 5 or a 2. Then the joker hand is turned over. The joker has attracted to it all of the remaining 5's and 2's that were in play.

Method: The top half of the pack is stacked. From the top down, the setup is X-4-5-6-X-X-4-5-6-3-2-X-3-Joker-5-5-6-X-3-A-2-X-X-3-A-2-4-6-4. The letter X indicates a random card and the letter A stands for ace. Place this portion of the deck on top of the rest of the deck. Case the deck until the time of performance.

When you're ready to do this trick, remove a die from the pocket. Let someone roll the die a few times to satisfy himself that the die is ordinary. As this is done, remove the deck from its case. Spread the cards face up between the hands. Remove the twenty-nine-card setup, and place the rest of the deck aside for the moment. Spread the twenty-nine-card setup from left to right, and remove the cards to the left of the joker with the left hand. Place this packet face down on the table to the left. Toss the joker out to the table. Place the balance of the setup face down on the table to the right.

Ask the spectator to roll the die and note the number on top. If the number rolled is a 1, 2 or 3, the spectator will remove cards of that value from the packet on the left. If the number rolled is a 4, 5, or 6, he will remove cards of that value from the packet on the right. Sometimes a packet will not have cards of the value rolled by the spectator. The trick will still work.

Say the spectator rolls a 5. Pick up the packet on the right, turn it face up and spread it on the table. Slide out all of the 5's from this packet. Do not disturb the order of the other cards in the spread. Close up the spread, turn this packet face down and place it in front of you. Ask the spectator to turn the die over. In our example, a 2 will now show. Spread the left-hand packet face up on the table. Remove any 2's that may be in this packet. Gather the cards and turn this packet face down.

Draw a line across the middle of the joker. Ask the spectator to place one of the chosen numbers above the line, the other number below the line. Drop the face-up joker on top of the right-hand packet. Drop the left-hand packet on top of the joker. Place the packet on top of the deck. The joker is the only face-up card in the deck.

The spectator deals five poker hands. One of them will contain the face-up joker. Turn each of the other hands face up to show an absence of 5's or 2's. Then turn the joker hand over to show that the joker mysteriously attracted 5's and 2's to that hand.

52. Poker with Dice

In a game of poker, a player needs a pair of jacks or better to start the betting. The magician shows how a pair of dice can locate the necessary cards. Besides the cards, the magician uses a pair of dice and a cup. The cup can be a coffee cup or an opaque plastic glass.

The spectator shakes the dice and tosses them to the table. Say the numbers thrown are a 2 and a 6. The total is 8, so he deals eight cards off the top of the deck into a heap on the table. He covers one of the dice with the cup. Assume that the covered die is the one with the 6 showing. The spectator is directed to turn the visible die over and note the new number. The visible die is the one with the 2 showing. When it is turned over, the new number is a 5. The spectator deals five cards off the top of the deck onto the tabled heap. The rest of the deck is placed aside.

Now the cup is removed. Whatever number shows on this die, the spectator picks up the tabled heap and deals that many cards into a new heap on the table. The die shows a 6, so the spectator deals a heap of six cards. There are now two heaps, one on the table and one in the spectator's hand. When the top card of each is turned over, they show a pair of jacks.

Method: Beforehand, secretly place a pair of jacks seventh and eighth from the top of the deck. Perform the trick exactly as written above, and the jacks will turn up no matter which numbers are rolled with the dice.

53. Triple Find

Most dice tricks use a single die or a pair of dice. However, this trick, based on the ideas of George Kaplan and John Scarne, makes use of three dice. The dice are placed under an inverted cup so the numbers are concealed for the moment. The spectator counts a random number of cards from the top to the bottom of the deck. The random number is reprogrammed to produce a new number, one that the magician could not anticipate. This new number is used to form two heaps of cards.

The top card of each heap is turned up. For good measure, the bottom card of the deck is also turned up. The cards might be a 2, a 3 and a 5. When the cup is lifted, the numbers showing on top of the dice are a 2, a 3 and a 5, exactly matching the chosen cards. The number chosen by the spectator is a free choice that need never be known to the magician, yet the outcome is infallible.

Method: The cards may be borrowed. You will also need three dice and a teacup or coffee mug large enough to hide the dice. Run through the deck to remove any jokers. As you do, remember the top card, and the cards that lie seventh and eighth from the top. Memorize the values. The suits don't matter. Say these three cards are a 2, a 3 and a 5. Close up the deck and place it face down on the table.

Remark on the fact that people come up with all kinds of systems for winning at dice and cards. Almost all such systems make use of numbers that are manipulated in various ways to guide the outcome. Ask the spectator to think of a number between 1 and 10, but not to tell anyone what it is. Explain that his number will be the basis for an unusual game with cards and dice.

Pretend to concentrate, as if you are getting telepathic signals from the spectator's mind. Turn the cup mouth down. Lift it at the inner end, and slide the dice under the cup one at a time, Figure 94. As each die is slid under the cup, turn it so it matches one of the numbers you have memorized. In our example, the dice would be slid under the cup and turned so the numbers 2, 3, 5 would be uppermost. Lower the cup over the dice.

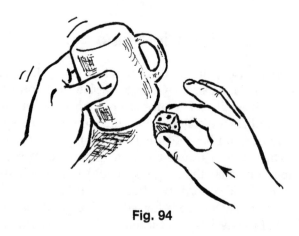

Fig. 94

Ask the spectator to think of a number *between* 1 and 10. He does not have to tell you the number. Let's say the number is 8. Have him transfer that many cards, one at a time, from the top to the bottom of the deck. When he has done this, remark that you are now going to show him how numbers are manipulated by system bettors. Have him double his number, add 2, multiply the result by 5, and finally, subtract 14. In our example, he would multiply 8 by 2 to get 16, add 2 to get 18, multiply by 5 to get 90, and then subtract 14 to arrive at the final number, 76.

Whatever the digit on the left, he transfers that many cards, one at a time, from the bottom to the top of the deck. In this case, he would transfer seven cards. Whatever the digit on the right, he deals that many cards into a heap on the table from the top of the deck. In our example, he deals a heap of six cards. The balance of the deck is placed next to the six-card heap.

Remove the top card of the six-card heap, and the top card of the balance of the deck. Place these two cards face up on the table in front of the cup. Then turn the larger packet of cards over. Three cards are now visible—the face card of the large packet and the other two cards. These cards will be a 2, a 3 and a 5. All that remains is to have someone lift the cup to reveal that the top numbers on the dice match the chosen cards.

54. The Lost Die

"I was going to do a trick with two dice, but one of them got lost. We'll use a real die and a drawing of a die." The magician draws a picture of a die on a piece of paper, and places it on the table alongside a real die, Figure 95. He turns his back and invites a spectator to roll the real die. Whatever number comes up, the spectator removes that many cards from the top of the pack. Say that a spectator named John rolls a 3 with the die. He would withdraw three cards from the pack.

The second spectator, whose name might be Jane, chooses a number and writes it on the drawing of the die. To make things interesting, her number should be different from the first number. Say the second number is 6. Jane removes six cards from the deck.

The two groups of cards are shuffled together, and the combined packet is spread face up on the table. John remembers the card at the position corresponding to the number he rolled. In this case, he would note the card that is third down from the top

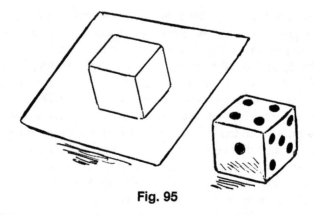

Fig. 95

of the packet. Jane remembers the card whose position corresponds to her chosen number. In this example, she would remember the card that is sixth from the top. The packet is gathered and handed to the magician. The magician is seated at the table, but he has turned his head to one side. "I shall try to cause your two cards to change places. To make it harder, I won't look at the cards."

This is accomplished as follows. Hold the packet in the left hand, deal the top card into the right hand, the next card on top of that, the next on top of that, and so on, reversing the order of the cards. When this has been done, silently transfer the top card to the bottom. This is the original bottom card, and it must be placed back on the bottom of the packet for the trick to work.

Place the packet on the table, and turn and face the audience. Deal the cards into a face-down row on the table, counting aloud as you do so. "There are nine cards, so we have the numbers from one to nine." There is a die on the table with the number 3 showing. "John, what was your card?" John replies that he chose the ♠J. "And Jane, what card did you pick?" Jane says that she picked the ♦Q.

"John, your card was third." Count to the third card and turn it face up. "But that's Jane's card." When the card is turned up it will be the ♦Q, the card chosen by Jane. "And Jane, what was your number?" Her number was six. Count to the sixth card. "The card at Jane's number is John's card." Turn the sixth card face up to reveal the ♠J.

Most people know that on a die the numbers run from 1 to 6. When you ask someone to write a number on the drawing of the die, they may misunderstand and think you want them to write any number. The trick will work no matter which number is chosen.

55. The Odds Against

A friend of mine does table magic in restaurants. He finds that tricks based on gambling themes tend to go over especially well. After I demonstrated the following routine, it became one of the tricks he uses on a regular basis. It is the handling I use for an ingenious trick invented by Howard Adams. All you need is a deck of cards and two dice. Five cards are going to be torn in half, so it is best to use an old deck of cards for this trick.

Remove the ♥A through ♥5 and arrange them in any order. The rest of the deck is not used. Turn the packet face down and tear it across the middle. This creates two packets of half-cards. Place one on top of the other. Invite the spectator to give the ten-card packet several straight cuts. Take back the packet and deal the top five half-cards into a heap on the table. Place the other heap alongside it without altering the order of the cards in this heap.

Place two dice in front of the spectator. "This is a trick with matching numbers. In order to get a match the first time, we have to beat odds of four to one. Arrange those two dice so the top spots total four." The spectator might arrange them with a 3 showing on one die, a 1 on the other. He places each die next to a packet. Pick up the packet next to the die showing a 3-spot. Openly transfer three half-cards from top to bottom, and replace this packet on the table. Pick up the packet next to the die showing the 1-spot. Openly transfer one half-card from top to bottom.

This next bit of handling is a display that is the key to the success of the trick. "Let's see how we did so far." Grasp a packet with each hand, Figure 96. Turn the packets face up, Figure 97. "Not so good." Turn each packet face down and place them on the table. Pick up the top half-card of each packet and place this face-down pair to one side.

"Whenever we fail, the odds go up. This time the odds against

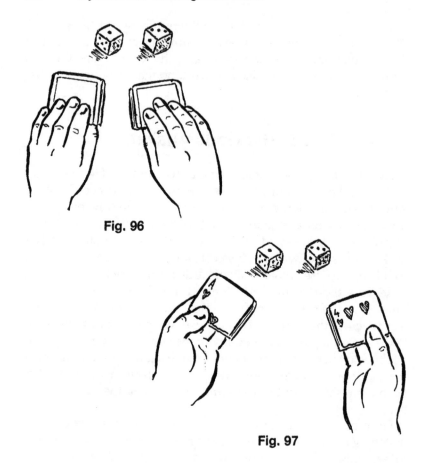

Fig. 96

Fig. 97

are seven to one. Arrange the two dice so the top numbers total seven." The spectator might arrange them with a 3 showing on one die, a 4 on the other. The spectator places a die next to each packet. Pick up the packet next to the 4-die and transfer four half-cards, one at a time, from top to bottom. Replace this packet on the table. Pick up the packet next to the 3-die and transfer three half-cards from top to bottom. Replace this packet on the table.

Grasp a packet with each hand, Figure 96 above, and turn the packets face up as in Figure 97 above. Once again, the cards don't match. "Still no luck." Turn the packets face down. Take the top half-card of each packet, and place this pair off to one side. The pattern repeats. On the next round, the odds are eight to one. The spectator arranges the dice so the top spots total 8. Transfer a total of eight half-cards from top-to-bottom, some from one heap, some from the other, according to how the spectator arranges the dice. Show that the face cards don't match. Take the top half-card of each heap and put this pair to one side.

On the last round the odds are nine to one. The spectator arranges the dice so the top spots total 9. Handle this step as you did the others, transferring a total of nine half-cards, but *don't* show the faces of the bottom cards of the packets. Pick up the top half-card of each heap and place this pair aside. There are four pairs of half-cards placed aside, and one pair of half-cards in front of the spectator. "This is the last chance to recoup our losses." Turn the half-cards up one at a time as you say (for example), "A red five and . . . the other half of the red five. We won." Pause for just a moment, then say, "And we won over here, and over here . . ." Now turn up the other pairs, showing a perfect match all the way through.

The use of two dice makes clear the many possible number combinations the spectator could choose from. The handling of Figure 96 and 97 sets up and reinforces the notion of failure right along; the audience sees that the cards aren't matching. At the finish, it comes as a surprise that non-matching pairs suddenly and inexplicably turn into matching pairs.

The handling given here is the way I do this trick. However, the reader may wish to consider a different handling of the trick, which is called "Make the Cards Match" and appears in my book *New Self-Working Card Tricks*.

X-RAY VISION

Kuda Bux, a magician from Kashmir, gained a worldwide reputation for his apparent ability to see while blindfolded. After layers of cloth had been applied in order to block his vision, he could duplicate writing made on a blackboard, hit a bull's-eye with a rifle shot, and pick out objects selected by audience members. On a more modest scale, the tricks in this chapter seem to demonstrate a similar ability to see objects hidden from view.

56. Illuminator

Sometimes inanimate objects can be made to give off a subliminal illumination. Though invisible to the naked eye, it can be detected with practice. The magician tests this proposition by having the spectator cover a die with a cup. Next, the magician reverses a card in the deck. When the cup is uncovered, the die is seen to show, say, the number 5; and when the spectator himself spreads the deck to reveal the value of the reversed card, it is also a 5.

In more detail, the spectator is given two dice, a cup and a deck of cards. The magician turns his head to one side so he can't see the action. The spectator drops the dice into the cup, shakes the cup and tosses the dice to the table. Whatever total is rolled with the dice, the spectator silently counts that many cards from the top of the pack into a heap on the table.

The spectator then covers one of the dice with the cup. This leaves one die in view. The spectator turns it over and notes the new number on top. Whatever it is, he counts that many additional cards off the deck onto the tabled heap. The magician now turns, faces the audience, and says, "It may be possible for me to deduce the number on the hidden die from the cards you just dealt. So, to eliminate that possibility, please put the heap back on top of the deck."

When this has been done, the magician takes the deck and lowers it beneath the table. "I don't want to see any cards. Just to be sure, I'll keep them out of sight, and pick a card that I think matches the number you threw with that hidden die." The deck is then brought into view. The cup is lifted. The number on the die may be 5. The spectator spreads the deck face down on the table. There is one face-up card in the deck and it is a 5-spot.

Method: Remove any ace through 6 in mixed suits from the deck. Arrange them in numerical order. Place this packet on top of the deck. The ace is the topmost card. Now transfer seven cards, one at a time, from the bottom to the top of the deck. This completes the preparation. The ace is now seventh from the top of the deck.

To present the trick, place the apparatus on the table. Turn your head to one side, and ask the spectator to roll the two dice and total them. He counts that many cards off the top of the deck into a heap. Then he covers one die. Instruct him that he can change his mind if he likes. Once he has decided on the die he wants covered, ask him to turn the other die over. He notes the number now showing on top of that die, and deals that many cards off the top of the deck onto the tabled heap.

Turn and face the spectator. Ask him to place the tabled heap on top of the deck. Now you have no clue as to the number showing on the hidden die. Take the deck below the level of the table-top or place the deck behind your back. Your task is simple. Turn the top card over so it is face up on top of the deck. Cut the deck and complete the cut. Bring the deck into view. Have the spectator lift the cup. A 5 might show on the die. Direct the spectator to spread the deck face down on the table. A 5-spot is face up in the center of the deck.

57. Mystery Sight

Some tricks create a sense of mystery because they are performed under conditions that seem to make cheating impossible. In "Mystery Sight" the apparatus is kept hidden, there are no gimmicks, yet the magician is able to bring the trick to a successful conclusion.

Four dice are used in this trick. They can be any four dice, but for clarity in the explanation, we shall assume that two of the dice are red and two are white. Also needed is a deck of cards and three cups. The cups can be coffee cups or paper cups.

The spectator shuffles the deck any way he likes. The magician then places the deck in his pocket where it remains until the end of the trick. While the magician turns his back, the spectator throws the dice a few times to satisfy himself that they are ordinary. He then arranges the two white dice so any total is uppermost. Let us say that he arranges the dice so that a 5 and a 3 are on top. The total is 8. The two white dice are covered with an inverted cup.

The spectator arranges the two red dice so that the same total is uppermost, but the two numbers need not be the same as on the white dice. We will say that the spectator chooses to arrange the red dice with a 6 showing on one die and a 2 on the other. The total is 8, the same as the total on the white dice. The spectator slides one of the red dice toward the magician. This die is covered with an inverted cup. He then turns the other die over to show a different number on top. Then he covers this die with the third cup.

The magician turns and faces the audience. On the table are three cups. One of them conceals two white dice. Each of the others conceals a red die. Tapping the cup nearest him, the magician says, "This is the die you chose to give to me. I'm going to see if I can guess the number on this die without lifting the cup." He concentrates a moment, then reaches into his pocket, removes a playing card and places it sight unseen on the table near the cup.

He points to the two cups near the spectator. "There are two dice in one of these cups and one die in the other. I'm going to make a guess as to the numbers showing on those dice." He reaches into his pocket, removes another card and places it sight unseen on the table next to his first card. "I chose these two cards for a reason. If their values are added to the value of the die you gave me, the total will be the same as the total of your three dice." The apparatus is uncovered. The magician is correct. The totals match.

Method: Before the trick begins, remove any 3-spot and any 4-spot from the deck. Place these two cards in your pocket. That is the only secret preparation.

To perform the trick, have the deck shuffled. Drop it into your pocket so that it goes under the two cards that were secretly placed in the pocket. In other words, the 3-spot and the 4-spot will be on top of the deck. Turn your head to one side. The spectator rolls the two white dice, remembers the total and covers the dice with the first cup. Say the dice show a 5 and a 3. The total is 8. He arranges the red dice so they total 8. Let's say that one die shows a 6 and the second die a 2. He slides one red die toward you and covers it with the second cup. Assume the die under this cup is the one with the 6 showing. He turns the other red die over and covers that die with the third cup. This red die will now have a 5 showing.

Turn and face the audience. The trick stands or falls on your ability to convince the audience that you have some sort of x-ray vision that allows you to see the numbers on the hidden dice. Stare at each cup in turn. Reach into your pocket and remove any card. Don't look at it. Stare at the back of the card. Stare at the cup in front of you. Shake your head. Return the card to the pocket. Look at the cups again. Reach into your pocket and remove the top card. Place it face down on the table.

Do the same thing with the second card. Lift the cup nearest to you. The die shows a 6. Turn your two cards over to reveal a 3 and a 4. Add 6 + 3 + 4 to arrive at a total of 13. The spectator now uncovers his three dice. The two whites will be a 5 and a 3. The red die will show a 5. Adding 5 + 3 + 5 gives a total of 13. The totals match.

58. Repeat Miraskill

The final two tricks in this chapter are designed to follow one another. The deck is stacked, but the cards are shuffled by the spectator over and over again. Performed together, they produce a convincing impression that the magician has the ability to see through solid objects.

While a spectator shuffles about half the deck, the magician writes a prediction on a joker. The spectator deals the cards in his packet two at a time. Matching reds go into one heap, matching blacks into a separate heap, and pairs that contain one red and one black card go into a discard heap. When the matching reds are counted and compared to the matching blacks, it is seen that the prediction was correct.

Using the same cards, the trick is repeated. The magician writes a new prediction. The spectator shuffles the packet, and again deals it into three heaps as before. There will be a new outcome. Nevertheless, the magician's prediction proves to be correct.

Method: Miraskill is a classic card effect created by Stewart James. The repeat version is the author's invention. The deck is stacked beforehand. This stack enables you to perform "Repeat Miraskill" and the next trick, "Eyeless Vision."

Prior to performance, remove four spades, twelve clubs, six diamonds and the ♥A from the deck. Shuffle these twenty-three cards together, and place them on the table. Place a joker on top of this heap, and then place the rest of the deck on top of all. Case the deck until the time of performance.

When you are ready to perform "Repeat Miraskill," remove the cards from the case. Remark that you want to write a prediction, and spread the cards so you can see the faces. Place the cards in front of the joker to one side on the table. This is the twenty-three-card packet containing the ♥A.

Take the joker off the face of the remaining packet, and hand the balance of this packet (twenty-nine cards in all) to the spectator. Ask him to shuffle it thoroughly. When he has done this, have him place it face up on the table. For this first trick to work, there must be a red card at the face of the packet. If there is, proceed to the next paragraph. If there is a black card at the face of the packet, request that the spectator give the packet a straight cut. There are more reds than blacks in this packet, so chances are good that after the cut, there will be a red card at the face of the packet. If not, ask him to give the packet another cut.

When you see that there is a red card at the face of the packet, place your hand palm down on the packet. Stare at the cards. Explain that by means of x-ray vision you can see down into the packet. After a moment, nod and take your hand away. On the face of the joker write, "EIGHT MORE REDS THAN BLACKS," and place the joker on the table, writing-side down.

Ask the spectator to turn the packet face down, and hold it in his left hand. He is to deal cards two at a time off the top. If the two cards are red, they go into one heap. If both cards are black, they go into a separate heap. If one card is red and one black, they go into a discard heap. When he has completed the deal, there will be one card left over. Direct him to toss it into the discard heap. Now, ask him to count the reds in the heap containing matching reds. He might get a total of twelve red cards. Then have him count the blacks in the black heap. He might get a total of four blacks.

"You have eight more reds than blacks." Turn the prediction card over to reveal exactly this same result.

Say, "I feel lucky. Let's try it again." The spectator gathers the twenty-nine cards, and shuffles them any way he likes. He then places the packet face up on the table. This time there must be a black card at the face in order for the trick to work. If there is, take this card and hold it in the left hand. If there is a red card at the face of the packet, direct the spectator to give the packet a cut. He then gives the cards a few cuts, however many are necessary to bring a black card to the face of the packet.

Take the black card into the left hand. Place your right hand palm down on the packet. As before, pretend to stare down into the cards as if you have special powers. Nod your head. On the face of the black card write, "TEN MORE REDS THAN BLACKS," and place the card writing-side down on the table. The packet now contains twenty-eight cards. Ask the spectator to hold the packet face down in his left hand. He deals cards off the top two at a time. If both cards are red, he deals them into one heap. If both are black, he deals them into a separate heap. If one card is black and one red, he deals them into a discard heap.

At the conclusion of the deal, ask him to count the number of reds. There may be sixteen reds. Then he counts the number of blacks. There may be six blacks. Say, "This time there are ten more reds than blacks." Turn over the prediction card to show you are correct.

It is not always easy to write on the face of a playing card with a pen or pencil. This is because playing cards are made from plastic-coated stock that will not accommodate hard lead pencils or ballpoint pens. You may find it works better to use a felt-tipped pen with a fine tip.

59. Eyeless Vision

You have just completed the performance of "Repeat Miraskill." This is a follow-up trick that seems to provide conclusive evidence that you have special powers. It is based on ideas of Ralph Hull and Bob Hummer. Hand the twenty-nine-card packet to a spectator. Ask him to give it several shuffles. Hand the remainder of the deck (the twenty-three-card packet) to another spectator for shuffling. When the cards have been mixed, place the larger packet face down on the table to your right. Place the smaller packet alongside it, to your left.

Turn your head to one side. Ask a spectator to lift off a group of cards from the right-hand packet. "Make it a small bunch of cards, no more than ten cards." Have the spectator turn this group of cards over so it is face up. He then places it on top of the packet to your left. Now have him lift off a larger bunch of cards from the left-hand packet. "Lift off more than ten cards, say somewhere between ten and twenty cards." When he has done this, ask him to turn this bunch of cards over and place it on top of the right-hand packet.

Turn and face the audience. Point to the right-hand packet and say, "Please give these cards a good shuffle." When he does this, the audience sees that he has mixed face-up and face-down cards together. Make sure he doesn't inadvertently turn the packet over. When he has shuffled the packet, place it on the table to your right. Say, "Let's really mix the cards," and turn the right-hand packet over. Then turn the left-hand packet over. Then turn the right-hand packet over once more. Riffle shuffle the two heaps together.

When the deck has been squared after the shuffle, cut it into two heaps. Turn the right-hand packet over. Then turn the left-hand packet over. Riffle shuffle the two heaps together. Square the deck and place it on the table in front of you. Turn your hand palm down, place it on top of the deck and say, "The face-up cards are too easy. I could have looked at them during the shuffle. Concentrating on the face-down cards, I see ten, fifteen, twenty, exactly twenty-three face-down cards. Please go through the deck. Remove the face-down cards and count them, but please leave them face-down."

The spectator does this, and verifies that there are exactly twenty-three face-down cards. Push the face-up cards to one side. Place the face-down packet before you, and cover it with your hand. Say, "Now we try for suit. The weakest signal is coming from the hearts. The strongest signal comes from the clubs. I see twelve clubs." Turn your head to one side so you can't see the faces of the cards. The spectator turns the packet face up and counts the number of clubs. There will be exactly twelve.

"Clubs gave off the strongest signal because there were so many of them. Hearts were weakest, and therefore more of a challenge to see clearly. Amidst all those cards, I did see that there was one heart, the ace of hearts. Was I correct?" The spectator looks through the packet and verifies that there is just one heart, and it is the ace.

CARD TO WALLET

Magicians like to produce selected cards from surprising locations. One of the classic tricks in this category is called the "card to pocketbook." As the title indicates, a card chosen by a spectator mysteriously vanishes from the deck and is found in a pocketbook or purse. Card expert John Scarne popularized this trick with the production of a signed card from his wallet. Scarne's method used advanced sleight of hand. Each of the tricks in this chapter use self-working methods to bring about a similar effect.

60. Prediction Wallet

In this trick, a freely chosen and signed card disappears from the deck and is found in the magician's wallet. In greater detail, a card is chosen, signed on the face and cut into the deck. Also contained in the deck is a piece of paper in the form of a prediction. The prediction is as shown in Figure 98. It says, "LOOK AT THE WALL."

The magician observes, "That's the problem with predictions. They're usually true, but no one knows what they mean. We're told to look at the wall, but we are not told which wall, or what exactly we are to look for. In the meantime, I'll try to find your card." The magician places the deck behind his back, struggles to find the chosen card and then gives up. The deck is placed on the table.

"See anything on the wall that looks like your card?" The spectator says no. Then the magician realizes that the prediction is not just a piece of paper, but a folded piece of paper. When the paper is unfolded, it looks like Figure 99. Now it says, "LOOK AT THE WALLET." "That makes more sense." The magician removes his wallet from his inside jacket pocket, and extracts a playing card. It is the signed card chosen by the spectator.

Method: Most card-to-wallet tricks demand sleight-of-hand ability. This version of the trick is much easier to perform than some, although a certain amount of agility is called for. It was devised by Don Nielsen and the author, and it is similar to a trick of Frank Chapman's. You must be wearing a jacket in order to perform this trick. If you are right-handed, the wallet should be in the inside jacket pocket on the left.

On a piece of paper slightly smaller in size than a playing card, write the prediction shown in Figure 99. Fold the right side of the paper back to form the partial prediction shown in Figure 98. Place the folded paper between two jokers. Then place the jokers inside the card box. Place the deck in the card box on top of the jokers.

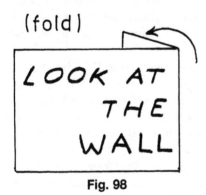

Fig. 98

Fig. 99

When you are going to perform a few card tricks, remove the deck, but leave the jokers behind. Do two or three tricks, then replace the deck in the card box so that the two jokers are on the bottom of the deck. Pretend that you just remembered another trick you wanted to perform. Remove the deck with the jokers on the bottom, and place the deck on the table. Invite the spectator to cut off about half the deck, shuffle it and place it on the table. He is to look at the top card and initial the face of this card. Then ask him to place this card on top of the shuffled packet. Put the rest of the deck on top of all. This maneuver positions the jokers directly on top of the chosen card.

You want to obscure the location of the chosen card. One way to do it is as follows. Cut about a quarter of the deck off the top and place it on the table. Put the rest of the deck on top of this packet. Then cut the deck in half and complete the cut. As you perform these maneuvers, say, "That should mix the cards." Next remark, "I had a prediction with me," and pat the pockets. "It just arrived in the mail from Swami Sebastian. Maybe it's here." Spread the deck between the hands until you get to the piece of paper. Cut the deck at this point and complete the cut so the paper is on top.

"Here it is. It makes no more sense now than it did when I first read it. If I can't find your card, I guess we can stare at the wall and see what happens." Place the deck behind the back as you speak. Transfer the top card (a joker) to the bottom of the deck. Take the new top card (the signed selection) and slide it under the jacket as far as it will go, in the direction shown in Figure 100. Press the left hand against the side, so the card is trapped in place under the arm.

(Rear View)

Fig. 100

Bring the right hand out from under the jacket. Take the deck with the right hand and place it on the table. Turn the top card of the deck face up and say, "I know you didn't choose this card because it isn't signed. What card did you pick?" The spectator names the card. Tap the prediction. "Now that I look at this piece of paper again, it appears to be folded in half. Unfold it and read it aloud." When the spectator does this, reach inside the jacket with the right hand. Take the chosen card and slide it into the wallet. Bring the wallet out into view. Remove the card and toss it out to reveal that the chosen card ended up inside the wallet.

61. Dracula's Calling Card

"Playing cards are symbols. The picture cards symbolize royalty, hearts represent romance. Diamonds are symbols for wealth. Best known is the ace of spades, called the death card, symbolic of bad news. The subject of this trick is the jack of spades. The black jacks symbolize vampires, and the jack of spades is known as the Dracula card."

As the above patter story is related to the audience, the magician removes his wallet from his pocket, opens it and shows that it contains a face-down playing card. The identity of this card is not revealed. "I keep Dracula here where there is no light." The wallet is closed and placed on the table.

"I'd like to show you how vampires kidnap their victims. It happens in the blink of an eye." The spectator chooses a card by a random process. That card might be the ♥4. Instantly the ♥4 changes into the Dracula card. The wallet is opened and the playing card removed. When it is turned face up, it is the card just chosen by the spectator, the ♥4.

Method: Beforehand, remove the ♥4 from the deck and place it inside the wallet. The only other preparation is that two groups of cards are going to be arranged in numerical order. This can be done in front of the audience, but the trick moves faster if the cards are arranged ahead of time. The arrangement is easy to remember. Stack the ♦A through ♦10 in numerical order, ace at the top, ten at the bottom of the packet. Arrange the ♥A through ♥10 in numerical order from the top down. In place of the ♥4 place the Dracula card, the ♠J.

It is necessary to explain to the audience that playing cards are symbolic of other things. In this connection, books on the subject of fortune-telling with cards are valuable sources of patter ideas. In many such books, the jacks are described as short-tempered troublemakers, untrustworthy persons, and insincere lovers. If a vampire is anything, he is an insincere lover. Having established that the ♠J is a vampire card, open the wallet and show that you have a card there. "I call this Dracula's tomb, the place where he takes his victims." Close the wallet and place it on the table near you.

"We're going to choose a victim for Dracula, but we are going to do it in a manner that is entirely left to chance." Hold the diamond packet face up in the right hand, the heart packet face up in the left hand, Figure 101. Drop the diamond packet onto the table. Spread the cards a bit to show that they are in numerical order. Square the diamond packet. Spread the first four or five face cards of the heart packet to show that they too are in numerical order. Don't spread to the ♠J. This card must be kept concealed until the finish of the trick. Square the heart packet and drop it face up on top of the diamond packet.

Pick up the combined packet, turn it face down and place it in

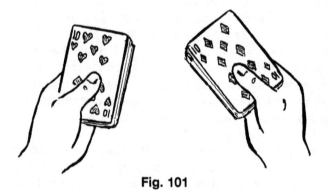

Fig. 101

the left hand. Say, "The cards are in order, so let's randomize them a bit." Push the top three cards off without reversing their order. Take them in the right hand and transfer them to the bottom of the packet. Now say, "I'd like you to pick a card. Say 'stop' anywhere among the first ten cards I deal." Push off the top card of the packet. Take it between the right thumb and first finger. Take the next card under it, the next under that, and so on until the spectator calls "stop." She can stop you at any time during the dealing of the first ten cards.

When "stop" has been called, put the right-hand packet on the table. Turn the top card of the left-hand packet face up, Figure 102. "This will be our marker." Drop it face up onto the tabled packet. Drop the balance of the left-hand cards on top of all. Then place the packet into the left hand. Push off the top ten cards without disturbing their order. Take this group in the right hand. Put the packets side-by-side on the table.

Deal simultaneously off the tops of the two packets. Turn each

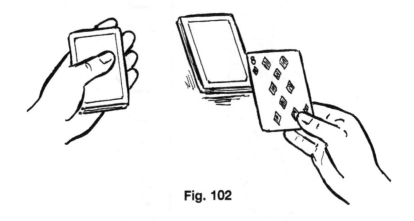

Fig. 102

of the right-hand cards face up. Deal each of the left-hand cards face down. Deal into vertical columns so the index corner of each face-up card is visible. Continue until you deal the marker card with the left hand. The card simultaneously dealt with the right hand is dealt face down. Pick up the remainder of the right-hand packet. Turn it face up and spread it below the cards on the right. The reason for doing this is to emphasize that the cards are in strict numerical order. The layout will look as shown in Figure 103.

Point out that the marker indicates that the chosen card will be the ♥4. The fact that the cards are in numerical order gives the appearance of honesty to the proceedings. Also, because the cards are in order, it is obvious at a glance that the face-down card between the ♥3 and ♥5 must be the ♥4.

Square up the right-hand packet. "Dracula has chosen a victim, the four of hearts. This is how fast the victim is spirited away to the castle." Tap the packet against the wallet. Spread the packet face up on the table. Slide out the face-down card. Pause for dramatic effect, then turn the card over to reveal the ♠J. Open the wallet. Slide out the face-down card. Turn it over to reveal the ♥4.

The performance of a trick like this gives you an excuse to

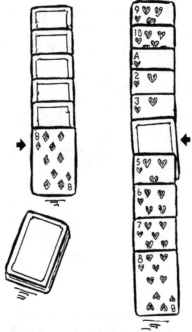

Fig. 103

make use of vampire jokes. For example, Dracula's favorite tourist attraction in New York City is the Vampire State Building. His favorite drink is tomato juice, his favorite card game cutthroat poker. Dracula's favorite song is "I Left Her Heart in San Francisco," and his favorite book is *In Cold Blood*.

62. The Mystery Card

The mysterious disappearance of a playing card produces a spooky effect. That outcome is achieved here in a novel way. The spectator is given the ♣A through ♣10. She moves a random number of cards from the top to the bottom of the packet. The magician removes a card from his wallet, places it on top of the packet and gives it a straight cut to bury the mystery card. The spectator again moves a random number of cards from the top to the bottom of the packet. The packet is then turned face up, and the cards dealt into a face-up row on the table. The cards are in order from ace to ten, and the mystery card is nowhere to be found.

Method: Before you begin the trick, remove the ♣10 and place it in the wallet. This should be done in secret before the performance.

"I carry a mystery card with me, a card given to me at a seance I attended long ago." Place the wallet on the table. As you speak, spread the deck so you alone can see the cards. Remove the ♣9 and place it at the face of the deck. Remove the ♣8 and place it on the ♣9. Continue this way, removing the cards in reverse numerical order down to the ace. At the end of this process, the ♣A will be the face card of the deck and the ♣9 the ninth card from the face.

Push over the face-most nine cards with the left thumb. Take this packet with the right hand, and put the balance of the deck on the table. Place the nine-card packet face down in the left hand and say, "I'm going to demonstrate the power of this mystery card with the ace through ten of clubs. First we should mix them a bit." You are going to apparently shuffle the cards. The "shuffle" is really a series of cuts. It is done as follows.

Elevate the packet to a vertical position in the left hand, Figure 104. Grasp the ends of the packet between the right thumb on one end, and the fingers on the other. Lift off the lower part of the packet with the right hand, Figure 105. The left thumb acts as a stop, holding back some of the cards. The right hand lifts its group of cards clear of the packet, and then drops this group on top of the balance of the packet, Figure 106. Repeat this sequence three or four times as you speak. It looks like the action of the overhand shuffle, but you are merely giving the packet a series of cuts.

As you hand the packet to the spectator say, "We are going to create a portal for the mystery card to enter. Please give the cards a cut. Good. Give them a second cut. Fine. One more for good luck." When the spectator has done this, instruct her to look at the top card of the packet. Let's say this card is a four. She returns the card to the top of the packet. Then she deals four cards, one at a time, from top to bottom. In other words, whatever the value of the chosen card, she transfers that many cards from top to bottom.

"Excellent. The entry portal has been created." Open your wal-

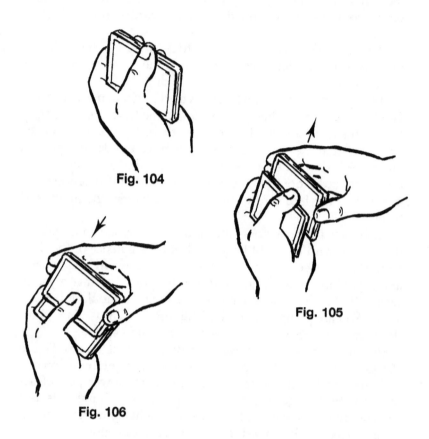

Fig. 104

Fig. 105

Fig. 106

let and remove the ♣10, but don't show the face of this card. Drop it on top of the packet, and ask the spectator to give the packet two or three straight cuts to bury the mystery card. "Now we need an exit portal. Please turn the top card over." Let's say this card is the ♣6. The spectator returns this card to the top of the packet. Because this card has a value of six, she transfers six cards from top to bottom.

"The mystery card has entered our world and left it. We started with the ace through ten of clubs. We finish with those same cards." Turn the packet face up. The ♣A will always be at the face of the packet. Deal the cards into a face-up row showing the ♣A through ♣10, and no sign of the mystery card.

63. Matchless Match Up

This version of the "card to wallet" routine is a little different because a surprise transposition occurs between two cards. The magician removes his wallet and places it on the table. The wallet has a couple of rubber bands around it to keep it secure and tamperproof. He says, "Before I left the house today, I placed a card in the wallet as a sort of prediction." The wallet remains in full view on the table all the way through this trick.

The spectator shuffles the deck. He chooses a card in a fair manner. Let's say the card is the ♠4. The magician says, "Isn't that a coincidence. You chose a black four, and the card I placed inside the wallet also happened to be a black four. Remove your card from the deck, and I'll remove my card from the wallet. That way we can show the perfect match."

The deck is spread face up on the table. The spectator looks for his card but can't find it. The magician says, "That's strange." He points to a card in the spread deck. "There's my card, the four of clubs. If my card is in the deck—" His voice trails off, but the implication is clear. He removes the rubber bands, opens the wallet and there is the spectator's chosen card, the ♠4.

The trick may be done at any time during the performance, but because of the surprise transposition of two cards, I have used it as a closing trick.

Method: The basis for this trick is an ingenious gimmick invented by Tom Sellers. Once the gimmick is made, it can be used over and over.

From a matching deck remove two jokers and the ♠4. Cut a quarter of the ♠4, and glue it to the back of one joker in the position shown in Figure 107. Turn the card over side-for-side, and place a pencil dot on the face of the joker in the position indicated in Figure 108. The dot corresponds to the location of the top of the ♠4 segment. This completes the preparation of the joker.

Place an ordinary joker face up on the table. Place the gimmicked joker face up on top of the first joker. Put these two cards in your pocket. To complete the preparation, place the ♠4 from the deck you intend to use in your wallet. Snap a couple of rubber bands around the wallet, and place it in the inside jacket pocket. The initial preparation takes a few minutes to complete, but once accomplished, the gimmick can be used over and over.

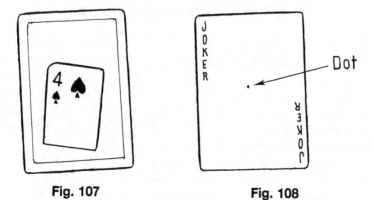

Fig. 107   **Fig. 108**

To present the trick, remove your wallet and place it on the table. Remark that you put a prediction card inside the wallet for safekeeping, but say nothing about the identity of this card. Ask someone to shuffle the deck. While this is being done, reach into the pocket that contains the jokers. Keep them squared as you bring them into view. Show them front and back. Drop them face up on the table, still squared. Take back the deck and spread it fanwise in the left hand, Figure 109. Make sure the center few cards are spread fairly wide apart from one another. Ask the spectator to indicate a card in the center of the spread.

Next say, "I want your card to remain securely in the middle of the deck, so we'll mark its location like this." The handling of the jokers now commences. It is easy to do, but care must be taken to follow the instructions *exactly*. Pick up the gimmicked joker. Don't show its back. Slide it into the deck directly to the right of the card chosen by the spectator, but do it in such a way that its

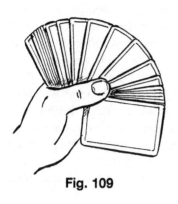

Fig. 109

left long-edge lines up with the left long-edge of this card, Figure 110. The pencil dot should line up with the top of this card. Pick up the other joker. Slide it on the left side of the chosen card, but such that its left long-edge lines up with the left long-edge of the chosen card, Figure 111. The chosen card is trapped and isolated between the jokers. To make it clear how the jokers are aligned with the card to

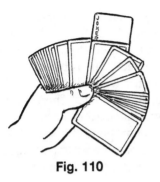

Fig. 110

Fig. 111

the right of each joker, the deck has been removed and just these four cards shown in Figure 112.

If the alignment is correct, when the deck is turned over, the audience sees the situation shown in Figure 113. The card the audience sees between the jokers is the ♠4. Call out its name, and then turn the deck face down again.

You are back to the situation shown in Figure 111. Slide the jokers out of the deck, and drop them into the pocket. Square up the deck, turn it face up. Place it on the table and say, "Amazingly enough, you chose a black four, and the card I put in my wallet before we started was also a black four. Let's remove our respective cards so we can verify the match."

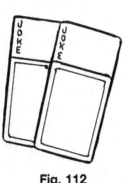

Fig. 112

Fig. 113

Spread the deck face up on the table. Invite the spectator to remove his card. Remove the rubber bands from the wallet, but take your time about it. Keep an eye on the spectator. Sooner or later, he will realize his card is not in the deck. The rubber bands should be off the wallet at this point, but the wallet is still closed. Look over the spread of cards. Spot the ♣4 and say, "There's my card, the other black four. Let's see now, if *my* card is in the deck, then *your* card—" It is not necessary to complete the sentence. The audience will make the connection. Open the wallet, remove the card and turn it over to reveal the spectator's chosen card.

64. Rapid Transit

The "card to wallet" routine also may be done in a comedy style where it appears that everything has gone wrong. That is the angle explored in this trick. The magician explains how a chosen card can end up in the magician's pocket, and then tries to demonstrate how it's done. Despite repeated tries, the chosen card refuses to leave the deck. All appears to be lost, but then an even more remarkable trick takes place: the card jumps to another pocket, then into the magician's wallet, and finally, into a sealed envelope in the wallet.

Method: The trick seems impossible, but it is easy to do. The starting point is a method worked out by Howard Wurst and Bill Pawson, and what it comes down to is the use of a duplicate card. The next time you purchase a deck of cards, buy two decks that are identical to one another. Use them interchangeably so both will show the same signs of wear. The result is that when a card is removed from one deck and placed in the other, it blends in and will not be suspected.

Decide on the card you want to appear in the wallet. Say it is the ♦A. Remove this card from one deck, seal it in a small envelope and place it in the bill compartment of your wallet. The type of envelope is not important to the working of the trick, but you may wish to use a small kraft envelope, also known as a coin or small parts envelope, available in office supply stores. The advantage to using this type of envelope is that it is just the right size to hold a playing card, so it does not take up much space in the wallet.

The deck the ♦A came from is returned to its case and put away. It will not be put to further use. The matching deck of fifty-two cards is the one you will use in this trick. Place a playing card from this deck in your left jacket pocket. The identity of this card is not important. Its face will not be seen, and it comes into play only as a ruse.

When ready to perform "Rapid Transit," cut the ♦A from this deck to the top of the deck. Place the deck on the table. Remark that you are going to explain one of Magic's most cherished secrets, the complete details of how a magician causes a playing card to leave the deck and appear in his pocket. Tap the left jacket pocket to indicate where the card is going to appear. The ♦A is going to be forced by a method called the X-force or cross-cut force. We will call the top half of the deck A and the bottom half B. Invite the spectator to cut off half the deck. This top half is placed alongside the bottom half, Figure 114. Pick up the bottom half (B), turn it sideways and place it on top of the other half. The result is shown in Figure 115.

It is necessary to divert attention away from the deck for the moment so the audience forgets which half is which. Call attention once again to the left jacket pocket. "First the magician empties his pocket." Remove loose change and keys from the pocket and place them on the table. Unknown to the audience, there is a playing card in the pocket. Next, lift off packet B. Pick up the top card of packet A and say, "Here's the card you cut to." Show it to the audience and ask them to remember this card. Replace it on top of packet A. Place packet B on top of all.

Give the deck two or three shuffles, followed by a cut. "First the magician has to secretly find your card." Hold the deck so

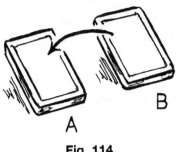

Fig. 114

Fig. 115

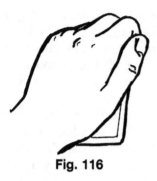

Fig. 116

you alone can see the faces of the cards. Remove the ♦A. Don't show the face of this card. "The magician palms the card and hides it in his pocket." Grip the card in a clumsy palm as in Figure 116. Place the card in the left jacket pocket. Pause for a moment and then add, "I don't do it that way."

Pretend to remove the palmed card from the pocket. Actually, you remove the card placed there earlier. Drop this card on top of the deck, give the deck a cut and complete the cut. This maneuver gets the ♦A out of the deck, and into your pocket where it will remain. Say, "Here's how I do it," and snap the fingers over the deck. Wave the hands over the deck. Reach into the left jacket pocket and fumble around. Bring the hand out empty. Behave as if the trick has failed.

"Let me try that again." Snap the fingers over the deck, wave the hands over the deck, reach into the left pocket, and again act crestfallen. Bring the empty left hand out. "Wait. Maybe it's supposed to be the other pocket." Reach into the right jacket pocket. Still no luck. Next say, "Of course. I forgot my own trick." Snap the fingers. Wave the hands over the deck. "It's not this pocket." Tap the left jacket pocket. "Or this pocket." Tap the right jacket pocket.

Grasp the left lapel with the left hand and say, "It's in *this* pocket." Use the right hand to point to the inside pocket. Reach into this pocket and withdraw the wallet. "And it's in *this* wallet." Open the wallet and withdraw the envelope. "And it's in *this* envelope." Put the wallet aside. "Which card did you choose?" The spectator names the ♦A. Tear open the envelope, withdraw the card and show it to be the very card chosen by the spectator, the ♦A.

65. Omega Card to Wallet

The aces and twos are removed from the deck and placed inside the card box for safekeeping. Removing his wallet from his pocket, the magician says, "I'm going to wager that I will be able to cause a freely chosen card to turn over by itself. If I'm wrong— it never happens, but in the unthinkable event that I am wrong— I'll give you the entire contents of my wallet." The spectator is then given a choice of either aces or twos. Let's say the choice is the aces. Next, he is given a choice of color, either red or black. Say the choice is red. Finally, he is given a choice of suit. There are two red suits, hearts and diamonds. Say the choice is hearts. The choice thus arrived at is the ♥A.

He removes the aces and twos from the card box and spreads them face down on the table. The ♥A has not reversed itself. The magician appears to be worried and exclaims, "That's never happened before. It's unthinkable!" The packet is turned face up and spread on the table. There should be four aces and four twos, a total of eight cards, but there are only seven, and the ♥A is missing. The spectator opens the wallet. The wallet is empty except for a single playing card, and that card is the missing ♥A.

Method: The card is forced by a method adapted from an idea of Mitsumatsu Matsuyama. Beforehand, empty the contents of your wallet. Remove the ♥A from the deck, seal it in a small envelope, and place the envelope into the bill compartment of the wallet. Close the wallet and place it in your pocket.

The trick may be presented at any time in the performance. When you are ready to perform it, hold the deck so you alone can see the faces of the cards. Spread the cards from hand to hand. Remove each ace and two as you come to them, and place each on the face of the deck. Do not call attention to what you are doing. The spectators can't see the faces of the cards. They know you are bringing certain cards to the face of the deck, but they don't know which cards these are.

When you have brought all of the aces and twos to the face of the deck (a total of seven cards), square the deck side-for-side. Hold the deck in the left hand, and push over the seven face-most cards of the deck. Take them with the right hand. Place the balance of the deck face down on the table. Spread the seven cards. Don't call attention to the number. Simply say, "I want you to pick a card, either an ace or a two. Until we know which card we're going to work with, I'll put them in the card box for safe-keeping. Nobody can tamper with these cards while they're stored away." Slide the seven cards into the card box, close the flap of the box and toss the box to the table.

"Too often people use psychological means to influence some-one's choice. To avoid such cheating, we're going to pick one of these cards purely by chance. Please cut a packet of cards off the deck. We're going to be doing this three times. To make sure we don't run out of cards, cut off about ten or so cards." It does not matter how many cards the spectator takes. I will go into detail on the process, so that the exact handling is clear.

"First we will decide whether the card is going to be an ace or a two. Place the top card under the packet and say 'ace.' Then deal the next card to the table and say 'two.' Then deal the next card under the packet and say 'ace.' Deal the next card to the table and say 'two.'" The spectator follows this procedure until the packet has been reduced to a single card. This card signifies ace, so the chosen card will be an ace.

"We know it's an ace, but we don't know which one. Aces come in two colors, red and black. Please cut another packet off the deck." The spectator does this. Have him transfer the top card to the bottom of the packet. As he does this, he says "Red." Direct him to deal the new top card to the table. As he does this, he says "Black." He transfers the top card to the bottom of the packet and as he does this, he says "Red." The next top card is dealt to the table as he says "Black." He continues the process until he has one card in hand. This card signifies red, so the chosen card will be a red ace.

"We're getting close. We know it's an ace and we know it's red. There are two red suits, hearts and diamonds. Please cut off another packet from the deck." The spectator does this. He then reduces the packet to a single card by the process described above, except that this time he says "Hearts, diamonds, hearts, diamonds," until the packet has been reduced to a single card. That card will signify hearts.

Say, "Our card is the ace of hearts, something we could not possibly have known in advance. Now let's perform the magic. I'm going to cause the ace of hearts to reverse itself inside the card box. I don't have to touch the cards or the card box to accomplish this amazing feat because of the powers vested in me by the Magicians Club of America." Snap your fingers over the card box, and have the spectator remove the cards and spread them face down on the table. There is no reversed card. The trick appears to be a failure. Have the spectator turn the cards face up so you can see what happened. Now it is discovered that the ♥A is gone. The spectator then opens your wallet and finds the missing ace.

The trick works because of the subtle force that is woven into the handling. If you say "Ace, two, ace, two," and so on as cards are alternately transferred from top to bottom and dealt to the table (a process known as "duck and deal"), you will always be left with a single card that corresponds to the first of the two words. In this example, "ace" is the first word that is said, so the final card will show up as you say "ace." This is true no matter how many cards the spectator starts with. If the duck and deal procedure is next done with the spectator saying, "Red, black, red, black," and so on until one card remains, he will say the word "red" as that final card shows up. The same force is at work when he says, "Hearts, diamonds, hearts, diamonds," and so on. Because "hearts" is the first word, he will arrive at "hearts" when the final card shows up.

A CATALOG OF SELECTED
DOVER BOOKS
IN ALL FIELDS OF INTEREST

A CATALOG OF SELECTED DOVER
BOOKS IN ALL FIELDS OF INTEREST

100 BEST-LOVED POEMS, Edited by Philip Smith. "The Passionate Shepherd to His Love," "Shall I compare thee to a summer's day?" "Death, be not proud," "The Raven," "The Road Not Taken," plus works by Blake, Wordsworth, Byron, Shelley, Keats, many others. 96pp. 5³/₁₆ x 8¼.   0-486-28553-7

100 SMALL HOUSES OF THE THIRTIES, Brown-Blodgett Company. Exterior photographs and floor plans for 100 charming structures. Illustrations of models accompanied by descriptions of interiors, color schemes, closet space, and other amenities. 200 illustrations. 112pp. 8⅜ x 11.   0-486-44131-8

1000 TURN-OF-THE-CENTURY HOUSES: With Illustrations and Floor Plans, Herbert C. Chivers. Reproduced from a rare edition, this showcase of homes ranges from cottages and bungalows to sprawling mansions. Each house is meticulously illustrated and accompanied by complete floor plans. 256pp. 9⅜ x 12¼.
        0-486-45596-3

101 GREAT AMERICAN POEMS, Edited by The American Poetry & Literacy Project. Rich treasury of verse from the 19th and 20th centuries includes works by Edgar Allan Poe, Robert Frost, Walt Whitman, Langston Hughes, Emily Dickinson, T. S. Eliot, other notables. 96pp. 5³/₁₆ x 8¼.   0-486-40158-8

101 GREAT SAMURAI PRINTS, Utagawa Kuniyoshi. Kuniyoshi was a master of the warrior woodblock print — and these 18th-century illustrations represent the pinnacle of his craft. Full-color portraits of renowned Japanese samurais pulse with movement, passion, and remarkably fine detail. 112pp. 8⅜ x 11.   0-486-46523-3

ABC OF BALLET, Janet Grosser. Clearly worded, abundantly illustrated little guide defines basic ballet-related terms: arabesque, battement, pas de chat, relevé, sissonne, many others. Pronunciation guide included. Excellent primer. 48pp. 4³/₁₆ x 5¾.
        0-486-40871-X

ACCESSORIES OF DRESS: An Illustrated Encyclopedia, Katherine Lester and Bess Viola Oerke. Illustrations of hats, veils, wigs, cravats, shawls, shoes, gloves, and other accessories enhance an engaging commentary that reveals the humor and charm of the many-sided story of accessorized apparel. 644 figures and 59 plates. 608pp. 6⅛ x 9¼.
        0-486-43378-1

ADVENTURES OF HUCKLEBERRY FINN, Mark Twain. Join Huck and Jim as their boyhood adventures along the Mississippi River lead them into a world of excitement, danger, and self-discovery. Humorous narrative, lyrical descriptions of the Mississippi valley, and memorable characters. 224pp. 5³/₁₆ x 8¼.   0-486-28061-6

ALICE STARMORE'S BOOK OF FAIR ISLE KNITTING, Alice Starmore. A noted designer from the region of Scotland's Fair Isle explores the history and techniques of this distinctive, stranded-color knitting style and provides copious illustrated instructions for 14 original knitwear designs. 208pp. 8⅜ x 10⅞.   0-486-47218-3

Browse over 9,000 books at www.doverpublications.com

CATALOG OF DOVER BOOKS

ALICE'S ADVENTURES IN WONDERLAND, Lewis Carroll. Beloved classic about a little girl lost in a topsy-turvy land and her encounters with the White Rabbit, March Hare, Mad Hatter, Cheshire Cat, and other delightfully improbable characters. 42 illustrations by Sir John Tenniel. 96pp. 5³⁄₁₆ x 8¼. 0-486-27543-4

AMERICA'S LIGHTHOUSES: An Illustrated History, Francis Ross Holland. Profusely illustrated fact-filled survey of American lighthouses since 1716. Over 200 stations — East, Gulf, and West coasts, Great Lakes, Hawaii, Alaska, Puerto Rico, the Virgin Islands, and the Mississippi and St. Lawrence Rivers. 240pp. 8 x 10¾. 0-486-25576-X

AN ENCYCLOPEDIA OF THE VIOLIN, Alberto Bachmann. Translated by Frederick H. Martens. Introduction by Eugene Ysaye. First published in 1925, this renowned reference remains unsurpassed as a source of essential information, from construction and evolution to repertoire and technique. Includes a glossary and 73 illustrations. 496pp. 6½ x 9¼. 0-486-46618-3

ANIMALS: 1,419 Copyright-Free Illustrations of Mammals, Birds, Fish, Insects, etc., Selected by Jim Harter. Selected for its visual impact and ease of use, this outstanding collection of wood engravings presents over 1,000 species of animals in extremely lifelike poses. Includes mammals, birds, reptiles, amphibians, fish, insects, and other invertebrates. 284pp. 9 x 12. 0-486-23766-4

THE ANNALS, Tacitus. Translated by Alfred John Church and William Jackson Brodribb. This vital chronicle of Imperial Rome, written by the era's great historian, spans A.D. 14-68 and paints incisive psychological portraits of major figures, from Tiberius to Nero. 416pp. 5³⁄₁₆ x 8¼. 0-486-45236-0

ANTIGONE, Sophocles. Filled with passionate speeches and sensitive probing of moral and philosophical issues, this powerful and often-performed Greek drama reveals the grim fate that befalls the children of Oedipus. Footnotes. 64pp. 5³⁄₁₆ x 8 ¼. 0-486-27804-2

ART DECO DECORATIVE PATTERNS IN FULL COLOR, Christian Stoll. Reprinted from a rare 1910 portfolio, 160 sensuous and exotic images depict a breathtaking array of florals, geometrics, and abstracts — all elegant in their stark simplicity. 64pp. 8⅜ x 11. 0-486-44862-2

THE ARTHUR RACKHAM TREASURY: 86 Full-Color Illustrations, Arthur Rackham. Selected and Edited by Jeff A. Menges. A stunning treasury of 86 full-page plates span the famed English artist's career, from Rip Van Winkle (1905) to masterworks such as Undine, A Midsummer Night's Dream, and Wind in the Willows (1939). 96pp. 8⅜ x 11. 0-486-44685-9

THE AUTHENTIC GILBERT & SULLIVAN SONGBOOK, W. S. Gilbert and A. S. Sullivan. The most comprehensive collection available, this songbook includes selections from every one of Gilbert and Sullivan's light operas. Ninety-two numbers are presented uncut and unedited, and in their original keys. 410pp. 9 x 12. 0-486-23482-7

THE AWAKENING, Kate Chopin. First published in 1899, this controversial novel of a New Orleans wife's search for love outside a stifling marriage shocked readers. Today, it remains a first-rate narrative with superb characterization. New introductory Note. 128pp. 5³⁄₁₆ x 8¼. 0-486-27786-0

BASIC DRAWING, Louis Priscilla. Beginning with perspective, this commonsense manual progresses to the figure in movement, light and shade, anatomy, drapery, composition, trees and landscape, and outdoor sketching. Black-and-white illustrations throughout. 128pp. 8⅜ x 11. 0-486-45815-6

Browse over 9,000 books at www.doverpublications.com

CATALOG OF DOVER BOOKS

THE BATTLES THAT CHANGED HISTORY, Fletcher Pratt. Historian profiles 16 crucial conflicts, ancient to modern, that changed the course of Western civilization. Gripping accounts of battles led by Alexander the Great, Joan of Arc, Ulysses S. Grant, other commanders. 27 maps. 352pp. 5⅜ x 8½. 0-486-41129-X

BEETHOVEN'S LETTERS, Ludwig van Beethoven. Edited by Dr. A. C. Kalischer. Features 457 letters to fellow musicians, friends, greats, patrons, and literary men. Reveals musical thoughts, quirks of personality, insights, and daily events. Includes 15 plates. 410pp. 5⅜ x 8½. 0-486-22769-3

BERNICE BOBS HER HAIR AND OTHER STORIES, F. Scott Fitzgerald. This brilliant anthology includes 6 of Fitzgerald's most popular stories: "The Diamond as Big as the Ritz," the title tale, "The Offshore Pirate," "The Ice Palace," "The Jelly Bean," and "May Day." 176pp. 5⅜ x 8½. 0-486-47049-0

BESLER'S BOOK OF FLOWERS AND PLANTS: 73 Full-Color Plates from Hortus Eystettensis, 1613, Basilius Besler. Here is a selection of magnificent plates from the *Hortus Eystettensis*, which vividly illustrated and identified the plants, flowers, and trees that thrived in the legendary German garden at Eichstätt. 80pp. 8⅜ x 11. 0-486-46005-3

THE BOOK OF KELLS, Edited by Blanche Cirker. Painstakingly reproduced from a rare facsimile edition, this volume contains full-page decorations, portraits, illustrations, plus a sampling of textual leaves with exquisite calligraphy and ornamentation. 32 full-color illustrations. 32pp. 9⅜ x 12¼. 0-486-24345-1

THE BOOK OF THE CROSSBOW: With an Additional Section on Catapults and Other Siege Engines, Ralph Payne-Gallwey. Fascinating study traces history and use of crossbow as military and sporting weapon, from Middle Ages to modern times. Also covers related weapons: balistas, catapults, Turkish bows, more. Over 240 illustrations. 400pp. 7¼ x 10⅝. 0-486-28720-3

THE BUNGALOW BOOK: Floor Plans and Photos of 112 Houses, 1910, Henry L. Wilson. Here are 112 of the most popular and economic blueprints of the early 20th century — plus an illustration or photograph of each completed house. A wonderful time capsule that still offers a wealth of valuable insights. 160pp. 8⅜ x 11. 0-486-45104-6

THE CALL OF THE WILD, Jack London. A classic novel of adventure, drawn from London's own experiences as a Klondike adventurer, relating the story of a heroic dog caught in the brutal life of the Alaska Gold Rush. Note. 64pp. 5³⁄₁₆ x 8¼. 0-486-26472-6

CANDIDE, Voltaire. Edited by Francois-Marie Arouet. One of the world's great satires since its first publication in 1759. Witty, caustic skewering of romance, science, philosophy, religion, government — nearly all human ideals and institutions. 112pp. 5³⁄₁₆ x 8¼. 0-486-26689-3

CELEBRATED IN THEIR TIME: Photographic Portraits from the George Grantham Bain Collection, Edited by Amy Pastan. With an Introduction by Michael Carlebach. Remarkable portrait gallery features 112 rare images of Albert Einstein, Charlie Chaplin, the Wright Brothers, Henry Ford, and other luminaries from the worlds of politics, art, entertainment, and industry. 128pp. 8⅜ x 11. 0-486-46754-6

CHARIOTS FOR APOLLO: The NASA History of Manned Lunar Spacecraft to 1969, Courtney G. Brooks, James M. Grimwood, and Loyd S. Swenson, Jr. This illustrated history by a trio of experts is the definitive reference on the Apollo spacecraft and lunar modules. It traces the vehicles' design, development, and operation in space. More than 100 photographs and illustrations. 576pp. 6¾ x 9¼. 0-486-46756-2

Browse over 9,000 books at www.doverpublications.com

A CHRISTMAS CAROL, Charles Dickens. This engrossing tale relates Ebenezer Scrooge's ghostly journeys through Christmases past, present, and future and his ultimate transformation from a harsh and grasping old miser to a charitable and compassionate human being. 80pp. 5³⁄₁₆ x 8¼. 0-486-26865-9

COMMON SENSE, Thomas Paine. First published in January of 1776, this highly influential landmark document clearly and persuasively argued for American separation from Great Britain and paved the way for the Declaration of Independence. 64pp. 5³⁄₁₆ x 8¼. 0-486-29602-4

THE COMPLETE SHORT STORIES OF OSCAR WILDE, Oscar Wilde. Complete texts of "The Happy Prince and Other Tales," "A House of Pomegranates," "Lord Arthur Savile's Crime and Other Stories," "Poems in Prose," and "The Portrait of Mr. W. H." 208pp. 5³⁄₁₆ x 8¼. 0-486-45216-6

COMPLETE SONNETS, William Shakespeare. Over 150 exquisite poems deal with love, friendship, the tyranny of time, beauty's evanescence, death, and other themes in language of remarkable power, precision, and beauty. Glossary of archaic terms. 80pp. 5³⁄₁₆ x 8¼. 0-486-26686-9

THE COUNT OF MONTE CRISTO: Abridged Edition, Alexandre Dumas. Falsely accused of treason, Edmond Dantès is imprisoned in the bleak Chateau d'If. After a hair-raising escape, he launches an elaborate plot to extract a bitter revenge against those who betrayed him. 448pp. 5³⁄₁₆ x 8¼. 0-486-45643-9

CRAFTSMAN BUNGALOWS: Designs from the Pacific Northwest, Yoho & Merritt. This reprint of a rare catalog, showcasing the charming simplicity and cozy style of Craftsman bungalows, is filled with photos of completed homes, plus floor plans and estimated costs. An indispensable resource for architects, historians, and illustrators. 112pp. 10 x 7. 0-486-46875-5

CRAFTSMAN BUNGALOWS: 59 Homes from "The Craftsman," Edited by Gustav Stickley. Best and most attractive designs from Arts and Crafts Movement publication — 1903–1916 — includes sketches, photographs of homes, floor plans, descriptive text. 128pp. 8¼ x 11. 0-486-25829-7

CRIME AND PUNISHMENT, Fyodor Dostoyevsky. Translated by Constance Garnett. Supreme masterpiece tells the story of Raskolnikov, a student tormented by his own thoughts after he murders an old woman. Overwhelmed by guilt and terror, he confesses and goes to prison. 480pp. 5³⁄₁₆ x 8¼. 0-486-41587-2

THE DECLARATION OF INDEPENDENCE AND OTHER GREAT DOCUMENTS OF AMERICAN HISTORY: 1775-1865, Edited by John Grafton. Thirteen compelling and influential documents: Henry's "Give Me Liberty or Give Me Death," Declaration of Independence, The Constitution, Washington's First Inaugural Address, The Monroe Doctrine, The Emancipation Proclamation, Gettysburg Address, more. 64pp. 5³⁄₁₆ x 8¼. 0-486-41124-9

THE DESERT AND THE SOWN: Travels in Palestine and Syria, Gertrude Bell. "The female Lawrence of Arabia," Gertrude Bell wrote captivating, perceptive accounts of her travels in the Middle East. This intriguing narrative, accompanied by 160 photos, traces her 1905 sojourn in Lebanon, Syria, and Palestine. 368pp. 5⅜ x 8½. 0-486-46876-3

A DOLL'S HOUSE, Henrik Ibsen. Ibsen's best-known play displays his genius for realistic prose drama. An expression of women's rights, the play climaxes when the central character, Nora, rejects a smothering marriage and life in "a doll's house." 80pp. 5³⁄₁₆ x 8¼. 0-486-27062-9

DOOMED SHIPS: Great Ocean Liner Disasters, William H. Miller, Jr. Nearly 200 photographs, many from private collections, highlight tales of some of the vessels whose pleasure cruises ended in catastrophe: the *Morro Castle, Normandie, Andrea Doria, Europa,* and many others. 128pp. 8⅜ x 11¾. 0-486-45366-9

THE DORÉ BIBLE ILLUSTRATIONS, Gustave Doré. Detailed plates from the Bible: the Creation scenes, Adam and Eve, horrifying visions of the Flood, the battle sequences with their monumental crowds, depictions of the life of Jesus, 241 plates in all. 241pp. 9 x 12. 0-486-23004-X

DRAWING DRAPERY FROM HEAD TO TOE, Cliff Young. Expert guidance on how to draw shirts, pants, skirts, gloves, hats, and coats on the human figure, including folds in relation to the body, pull and crush, action folds, creases, more. Over 200 drawings. 48pp. 8¼ x 11. 0-486-45591-2

DUBLINERS, James Joyce. A fine and accessible introduction to the work of one of the 20th century's most influential writers, this collection features 15 tales, including a masterpiece of the short-story genre, "The Dead." 160pp. 5³⁄₁₆ x 8¼. 0-486-26870-5

EASY-TO-MAKE POP-UPS, Joan Irvine. Illustrated by Barbara Reid. Dozens of wonderful ideas for three-dimensional paper fun — from holiday greeting cards with moving parts to a pop-up menagerie. Easy-to-follow, illustrated instructions for more than 30 projects. 299 black-and-white illustrations. 96pp. 8⅜ x 11. 0-486-44622-0

EASY-TO-MAKE STORYBOOK DOLLS: A "Novel" Approach to Cloth Dollmaking, Sherralyn St. Clair. Favorite fictional characters come alive in this unique beginner's dollmaking guide. Includes patterns for Pollyanna, Dorothy from *The Wonderful Wizard of Oz,* Mary of *The Secret Garden,* plus easy-to-follow instructions, 263 black-and-white illustrations, and an 8-page color insert. 112pp. 8¼ x 11. 0-486-47360-0

EINSTEIN'S ESSAYS IN SCIENCE, Albert Einstein. Speeches and essays in accessible, everyday language profile influential physicists such as Niels Bohr and Isaac Newton. They also explore areas of physics to which the author made major contributions. 128pp. 5 x 8. 0-486-47011-3

EL DORADO: Further Adventures of the Scarlet Pimpernel, Baroness Orczy. A popular sequel to *The Scarlet Pimpernel,* this suspenseful story recounts the Pimpernel's attempts to rescue the Dauphin from imprisonment during the French Revolution. An irresistible blend of intrigue, period detail, and vibrant characterizations. 352pp. 5³⁄₁₆ x 8¼. 0-486-44026-5

ELEGANT SMALL HOMES OF THE TWENTIES: 99 Designs from a Competition, Chicago Tribune. Nearly 100 designs for five- and six-room houses feature New England and Southern colonials, Normandy cottages, stately Italianate dwellings, and other fascinating snapshots of American domestic architecture of the 1920s. 112pp. 9 x 12. 0-486-46910-7

THE ELEMENTS OF STYLE: The Original Edition, William Strunk, Jr. This is the book that generations of writers have relied upon for timeless advice on grammar, diction, syntax, and other essentials. In concise terms, it identifies the principal requirements of proper style and common errors. 64pp. 5⅜ x 8¼. 0-486-44798-7

THE ELUSIVE PIMPERNEL, Baroness Orczy. Robespierre's revolutionaries find their wicked schemes thwarted by the heroic Pimpernel — Sir Percival Blakeney. In this thrilling sequel, Chauvelin devises a plot to eliminate the Pimpernel and his wife. 272pp. 5³⁄₁₆ x 8¼. 0-486-45464-9

Browse over 9,000 books at www.doverpublications.com

AN ENCYCLOPEDIA OF BATTLES: Accounts of Over 1,560 Battles from 1479 B.C. to the Present, David Eggenberger. Essential details of every major battle in recorded history from the first battle of Megiddo in 1479 B.C. to Grenada in 1984. List of battle maps. 99 illustrations. 544pp. 6½ x 9¼. 0-486-24913-1

ENCYCLOPEDIA OF EMBROIDERY STITCHES, INCLUDING CREWEL, Marion Nichols. Precise explanations and instructions, clearly illustrated, on how to work chain, back, cross, knotted, woven stitches, and many more — 178 in all, including Cable Outline, Whipped Satin, and Eyelet Buttonhole. Over 1400 illustrations. 219pp. 8⅜ x 11¼. 0-486-22929-7

ENTER JEEVES: 15 Early Stories, P. G. Wodehouse. Splendid collection contains first 8 stories featuring Bertie Wooster, the deliciously dim aristocrat and Jeeves, his brainy, imperturbable manservant. Also, the complete Reggie Pepper (Bertie's prototype) series. 288pp. 5⅜ x 8½. 0-486-29717-9

ERIC SLOANE'S AMERICA: Paintings in Oil, Michael Wigley. With a Foreword by Mimi Sloane. Eric Sloane's evocative oils of America's landscape and material culture shimmer with immense historical and nostalgic appeal. This original hardcover collection gathers nearly a hundred of his finest paintings, with subjects ranging from New England to the American Southwest. 128pp. 10⅝ x 9. 0-486-46525-X

ETHAN FROME, Edith Wharton. Classic story of wasted lives, set against a bleak New England background. Superbly delineated characters in a hauntingly grim tale of thwarted love. Considered by many to be Wharton's masterpiece. 96pp. 5³⁄₁₆ x 8 ¼. 0-486-26690-7

THE EVERLASTING MAN, G. K. Chesterton. Chesterton's view of Christianity — as a blend of philosophy and mythology, satisfying intellect and spirit — applies to his brilliant book, which appeals to readers' heads as well as their hearts. 288pp. 5⅜ x 8½. 0-486-46036-3

THE FIELD AND FOREST HANDY BOOK, Daniel Beard. Written by a co-founder of the Boy Scouts, this appealing guide offers illustrated instructions for building kites, birdhouses, boats, igloos, and other fun projects, plus numerous helpful tips for campers. 448pp. 5³⁄₁₆ x 8¼. 0-486-46191-2

FINDING YOUR WAY WITHOUT MAP OR COMPASS, Harold Gatty. Useful, instructive manual shows would-be explorers, hikers, bikers, scouts, sailors, and survivalists how to find their way outdoors by observing animals, weather patterns, shifting sands, and other elements of nature. 288pp. 5⅜ x 8½. 0-486-40613-X

FIRST FRENCH READER: A Beginner's Dual-Language Book, Edited and Translated by Stanley Appelbaum. This anthology introduces 50 legendary writers — Voltaire, Balzac, Baudelaire, Proust, more — through passages from *The Red and the Black, Les Misérables, Madame Bovary,* and other classics. Original French text plus English translation on facing pages. 240pp. 5⅜ x 8½. 0-486-46178-5

FIRST GERMAN READER: A Beginner's Dual-Language Book, Edited by Harry Steinhauer. Specially chosen for their power to evoke German life and culture, these short, simple readings include poems, stories, essays, and anecdotes by Goethe, Hesse, Heine, Schiller, and others. 224pp. 5⅜ x 8½. 0-486-46179-3

FIRST SPANISH READER: A Beginner's Dual-Language Book, Angel Flores. Delightful stories, other material based on works of Don Juan Manuel, Luis Taboada, Ricardo Palma, other noted writers. Complete faithful English translations on facing pages. Exercises. 176pp. 5⅜ x 8½. 0-486-25810-6

FIVE ACRES AND INDEPENDENCE, Maurice G. Kains. Great back-to-the-land classic explains basics of self-sufficient farming. The one book to get. 95 illustrations. 397pp. 5⅜ x 8½.
0-486-20974-1

FLAGG'S SMALL HOUSES: Their Economic Design and Construction, 1922, Ernest Flagg. Although most famous for his skyscrapers, Flagg was also a proponent of the well-designed single-family dwelling. His classic treatise features innovations that save space, materials, and cost. 526 illustrations. 160pp. 9⅜ x 12¼.
0-486-45197-6

FLATLAND: A Romance of Many Dimensions, Edwin A. Abbott. Classic of science (and mathematical) fiction — charmingly illustrated by the author — describes the adventures of A. Square, a resident of Flatland, in Spaceland (three dimensions), Lineland (one dimension), and Pointland (no dimensions). 96pp. 5³⁄₁₆ x 8¼.
0-486-27263-X

FRANKENSTEIN, Mary Shelley. The story of Victor Frankenstein's monstrous creation and the havoc it caused has enthralled generations of readers and inspired countless writers of horror and suspense. With the author's own 1831 introduction. 176pp. 5³⁄₁₆ x 8¼.
0-486-28211-2

THE GARGOYLE BOOK: 572 Examples from Gothic Architecture, Lester Burbank Bridaham. Dispelling the conventional wisdom that French Gothic architectural flourishes were born of despair or gloom, Bridaham reveals the whimsical nature of these creations and the ingenious artisans who made them. 572 illustrations. 224pp. 8⅜ x 11.
0-486-44754-5

THE GIFT OF THE MAGI AND OTHER SHORT STORIES, O. Henry. Sixteen captivating stories by one of America's most popular storytellers. Included are such classics as "The Gift of the Magi," "The Last Leaf," and "The Ransom of Red Chief." Publisher's Note. 96pp. 5³⁄₁₆ x 8¼.
0-486-27061-0

THE GOETHE TREASURY: Selected Prose and Poetry, Johann Wolfgang von Goethe. Edited, Selected, and with an Introduction by Thomas Mann. In addition to his lyric poetry, Goethe wrote travel sketches, autobiographical studies, essays, letters, and proverbs in rhyme and prose. This collection presents outstanding examples from each genre. 368pp. 5⅜ x 8½.
0-486-44780-4

GREAT EXPECTATIONS, Charles Dickens. Orphaned Pip is apprenticed to the dirty work of the forge but dreams of becoming a gentleman — and one day finds himself in possession of "great expectations." Dickens' finest novel. 400pp. 5³⁄₁₆ x 8¼.
0-486-41586-4

GREAT WRITERS ON THE ART OF FICTION: From Mark Twain to Joyce Carol Oates, Edited by James Daley. An indispensable source of advice and inspiration, this anthology features essays by Henry James, Kate Chopin, Willa Cather, Sinclair Lewis, Jack London, Raymond Chandler, Raymond Carver, Eudora Welty, and Kurt Vonnegut, Jr. 192pp. 5⅜ x 8½.
0-486-45128-3

HAMLET, William Shakespeare. The quintessential Shakespearean tragedy, whose highly charged confrontations and anguished soliloquies probe depths of human feeling rarely sounded in any art. Reprinted from an authoritative British edition complete with illuminating footnotes. 128pp. 5³⁄₁₆ x 8¼.   0-486-27278-8

THE HAUNTED HOUSE, Charles Dickens. A Yuletide gathering in an eerie country retreat provides the backdrop for Dickens and his friends — including Elizabeth Gaskell and Wilkie Collins — who take turns spinning supernatural yarns. 144pp. 5⅜ x 8½.
0-486-46309-5

HEART OF DARKNESS, Joseph Conrad. Dark allegory of a journey up the Congo River and the narrator's encounter with the mysterious Mr. Kurtz. Masterly blend of adventure, character study, psychological penetration. For many, Conrad's finest, most enigmatic story. 80pp. 5³⁄₁₆ x 8¼. 0-486-26464-5

HENSON AT THE NORTH POLE, Matthew A. Henson. This thrilling memoir by the heroic African-American who was Peary's companion through two decades of Arctic exploration recounts a tale of danger, courage, and determination. "Fascinating and exciting." — *Commonweal*. 128pp. 5⅜ x 8½. 0-486-45472-X

HISTORIC COSTUMES AND HOW TO MAKE THEM, Mary Fernald and E. Shenton. Practical, informative guidebook shows how to create everything from short tunics worn by Saxon men in the fifth century to a lady's bustle dress of the late 1800s. 81 illustrations. 176pp. 5⅜ x 8½. 0-486-44906-8

THE HOUND OF THE BASKERVILLES, Arthur Conan Doyle. A deadly curse in the form of a legendary ferocious beast continues to claim its victims from the Baskerville family until Holmes and Watson intervene. Often called the best detective story ever written. 128pp. 5³⁄₁₆ x 8¼. 0-486-28214-7

THE HOUSE BEHIND THE CEDARS, Charles W. Chesnutt. Originally published in 1900, this groundbreaking novel by a distinguished African-American author recounts the drama of a brother and sister who "pass for white" during the dangerous days of Reconstruction. 208pp. 5⅜ x 8½. 0-486-46144-0

THE HUMAN FIGURE IN MOTION, Eadweard Muybridge. The 4,789 photographs in this definitive selection show the human figure — models almost all undraped — engaged in over 160 different types of action: running, climbing stairs, etc. 390pp. 7⅞ x 10⅝. 0-486-20204-6

THE IMPORTANCE OF BEING EARNEST, Oscar Wilde. Wilde's witty and buoyant comedy of manners, filled with some of literature's most famous epigrams, reprinted from an authoritative British edition. Considered Wilde's most perfect work. 64pp. 5³⁄₁₆ x 8¼. 0-486-26478-5

THE INFERNO, Dante Alighieri. Translated and with notes by Henry Wadsworth Longfellow. The first stop on Dante's famous journey from Hell to Purgatory to Paradise, this 14th-century allegorical poem blends vivid and shocking imagery with graceful lyricism. Translated by the beloved 19th-century poet, Henry Wadsworth Longfellow. 256pp. 5³⁄₁₆ x 8¼. 0-486-44288-8

JANE EYRE, Charlotte Brontë. Written in 1847, *Jane Eyre* tells the tale of an orphan girl's progress from the custody of cruel relatives to an oppressive boarding school and its culmination in a troubled career as a governess. 448pp. 5³⁄₁₆ x 8¼. 0-486-42449-9

JAPANESE WOODBLOCK FLOWER PRINTS, Tanigami Kônan. Extraordinary collection of Japanese woodblock prints by a well-known artist features 120 plates in brilliant color. Realistic images from a rare edition include daffodils, tulips, and other familiar and unusual flowers. 128pp. 11 x 8¼. 0-486-46442-3

JEWELRY MAKING AND DESIGN, Augustus F. Rose and Antonio Cirino. Professional secrets of jewelry making are revealed in a thorough, practical guide. Over 200 illustrations. 306pp. 5⅜ x 8½. 0-486-21750-7

JULIUS CAESAR, William Shakespeare. Great tragedy based on Plutarch's account of the lives of Brutus, Julius Caesar and Mark Antony. Evil plotting, ringing oratory, high tragedy with Shakespeare's incomparable insight, dramatic power. Explanatory footnotes. 96pp. 5³⁄₁₆ x 8¼. 0-486-26876-4

Browse over 9,000 books at www.doverpublications.com

THE JUNGLE, Upton Sinclair. 1906 bestseller shockingly reveals intolerable labor practices and working conditions in the Chicago stockyards as it tells the grim story of a Slavic family that emigrates to America full of optimism but soon faces despair. 320pp. $5\frac{3}{16} \times 8\frac{1}{4}$. 0-486-41923-1

THE KINGDOM OF GOD IS WITHIN YOU, Leo Tolstoy. The soul-searching book that inspired Gandhi to embrace the concept of passive resistance, Tolstoy's 1894 polemic clearly outlines a radical, well-reasoned revision of traditional Christian thinking. 352pp. $5\frac{3}{16} \times 8\frac{1}{4}$. 0-486-45138-0

THE LADY OR THE TIGER?: and Other Logic Puzzles, Raymond M. Smullyan. Created by a renowned puzzle master, these whimsically themed challenges involve paradoxes about probability, time, and change; metapuzzles; and self-referentiality. Nineteen chapters advance in difficulty from relatively simple to highly complex. 1982 edition. 240pp. $5\frac{3}{8} \times 8\frac{1}{2}$. 0-486-47027-X

LEAVES OF GRASS: The Original 1855 Edition, Walt Whitman. Whitman's immortal collection includes some of the greatest poems of modern times, including his masterpiece, "Song of Myself." Shattering standard conventions, it stands as an unabashed celebration of body and nature. 128pp. $5\frac{3}{16} \times 8\frac{1}{4}$. 0-486-45676-5

LES MISÉRABLES, Victor Hugo. Translated by Charles E. Wilbour. Abridged by James K. Robinson. A convict's heroic struggle for justice and redemption plays out against a fiery backdrop of the Napoleonic wars. This edition features the excellent original translation and a sensitive abridgment. 304pp. $6\frac{1}{8} \times 9\frac{1}{4}$. 0-486-45789-3

LILITH: A Romance, George MacDonald. In this novel by the father of fantasy literature, a man travels through time to meet Adam and Eve and to explore humanity's fall from grace and ultimate redemption. 240pp. $5\frac{3}{8} \times 8\frac{1}{2}$. 0-486-46818-6

THE LOST LANGUAGE OF SYMBOLISM, Harold Bayley. This remarkable book reveals the hidden meaning behind familiar images and words, from the origins of Santa Claus to the fleur-de-lys, drawing from mythology, folklore, religious texts, and fairy tales. 1,418 illustrations. 784pp. $5\frac{3}{8} \times 8\frac{1}{2}$. 0-486-44787-1

MACBETH, William Shakespeare. A Scottish nobleman murders the king in order to succeed to the throne. Tortured by his conscience and fearful of discovery, he becomes tangled in a web of treachery and deceit that ultimately spells his doom. 96pp. $5\frac{3}{16} \times 8\frac{1}{4}$. 0-486-27802-6

MAKING AUTHENTIC CRAFTSMAN FURNITURE: Instructions and Plans for 62 Projects, Gustav Stickley. Make authentic reproductions of handsome, functional, durable furniture: tables, chairs, wall cabinets, desks, a hall tree, and more. Construction plans with drawings, schematics, dimensions, and lumber specs reprinted from 1900s *The Craftsman* magazine. 128pp. $8\frac{1}{8} \times 11$. 0-486-25000-8

MATHEMATICS FOR THE NONMATHEMATICIAN, Morris Kline. Erudite and entertaining overview follows development of mathematics from ancient Greeks to present. Topics include logic and mathematics, the fundamental concept, differential calculus, probability theory, much more. Exercises and problems. 641pp. $5\frac{3}{8} \times 8\frac{1}{2}$. 0-486-24823-2

MEMOIRS OF AN ARABIAN PRINCESS FROM ZANZIBAR, Emily Ruete. This 19th-century autobiography offers a rare inside look at the society surrounding a sultan's palace. A real-life princess in exile recalls her vanished world of harems, slave trading, and court intrigues. 288pp. $5\frac{3}{8} \times 8\frac{1}{2}$. 0-486-47121-7

THE METAMORPHOSIS AND OTHER STORIES, Franz Kafka. Excellent new English translations of title story (considered by many critics Kafka's most perfect work), plus "The Judgment," "In the Penal Colony," "A Country Doctor," and "A Report to an Academy." Note. 96pp. 5³⁄₁₆ x 8¼. 0-486-29030-1

MICROSCOPIC ART FORMS FROM THE PLANT WORLD, R. Anheisser. From undulating curves to complex geometrics, a world of fascinating images abound in this classic, illustrated survey of microscopic plants. Features 400 detailed illustrations of nature's minute but magnificent handiwork. The accompanying CD-ROM includes all of the images in the book. 128pp. 9 x 9. 0-486-46013-4

A MIDSUMMER NIGHT'S DREAM, William Shakespeare. Among the most popular of Shakespeare's comedies, this enchanting play humorously celebrates the vagaries of love as it focuses upon the intertwined romances of several pairs of lovers. Explanatory footnotes. 80pp. 5³⁄₁₆ x 8¼. 0-486-27067-X

THE MONEY CHANGERS, Upton Sinclair. Originally published in 1908, this cautionary novel from the author of *The Jungle* explores corruption within the American system as a group of power brokers joins forces for personal gain, triggering a crash on Wall Street. 192pp. 5⅜ x 8½. 0-486-46917-4

THE MOST POPULAR HOMES OF THE TWENTIES, William A. Radford. With a New Introduction by Daniel D. Reiff. Based on a rare 1925 catalog, this architectural showcase features floor plans, construction details, and photos of 26 homes, plus articles on entrances, porches, garages, and more. 250 illustrations, 21 color plates. 176pp. 8⅜ x 11. 0-486-47028-8

MY 66 YEARS IN THE BIG LEAGUES, Connie Mack. With a New Introduction by Rich Westcott. A Founding Father of modern baseball, Mack holds the record for most wins — and losses — by a major league manager. Enhanced by 70 photographs, his warmhearted autobiography is populated by many legends of the game. 288pp. 5⅜ x 8½. 0-486-47184-5

NARRATIVE OF THE LIFE OF FREDERICK DOUGLASS, Frederick Douglass. Douglass's graphic depictions of slavery, harrowing escape to freedom, and life as a newspaper editor, eloquent orator, and impassioned abolitionist. 96pp. 5³⁄₁₆ x 8¼. 0-486-28499-9

THE NIGHTLESS CITY: Geisha and Courtesan Life in Old Tokyo, J. E. de Becker. This unsurpassed study from 100 years ago ventured into Tokyo's red-light district to survey geisha and courtesan life and offer meticulous descriptions of training, dress, social hierarchy, and erotic practices. 49 black-and-white illustrations; 2 maps. 496pp. 5⅜ x 8½. 0-486-45563-7

THE ODYSSEY, Homer. Excellent prose translation of ancient epic recounts adventures of the homeward-bound Odysseus. Fantastic cast of gods, giants, cannibals, sirens, other supernatural creatures — true classic of Western literature. 256pp. 5³⁄₁₆ x 8¼. 0-486-40654-7

OEDIPUS REX, Sophocles. Landmark of Western drama concerns the catastrophe that ensues when King Oedipus discovers he has inadvertently killed his father and married his mother. Masterly construction, dramatic irony. Explanatory footnotes. 64pp. 5³⁄₁₆ x 8¼. 0-486-26877-2

ONCE UPON A TIME: The Way America Was, Eric Sloane. Nostalgic text and drawings brim with gentle philosophies and descriptions of how we used to live — self-sufficiently — on the land, in homes, and among the things built by hand. 44 line illustrations. 64pp. 8⅜ x 11. 0-486-44411-2

CATALOG OF DOVER BOOKS

ONE OF OURS, Willa Cather. The Pulitzer Prize–winning novel about a young Nebraskan looking for something to believe in. Alienated from his parents, rejected by his wife, he finds his destiny on the bloody battlefields of World War I. 352pp. 5³⁄₁₆ x 8¼. 0-486-45599-8

ORIGAMI YOU CAN USE: 27 Practical Projects, Rick Beech. Origami models can be more than decorative, and this unique volume shows how! The 27 practical projects include a CD case, frame, napkin ring, and dish. Easy instructions feature 400 two-color illustrations. 96pp. 8¼ x 11. 0-486-47057-1

OTHELLO, William Shakespeare. Towering tragedy tells the story of a Moorish general who earns the enmity of his ensign Iago when he passes him over for a promotion. Masterly portrait of an archvillain. Explanatory footnotes. 112pp. 5³⁄₁₆ x 8¼. 0-486-29097-2

PARADISE LOST, John Milton. Notes by John A. Himes. First published in 1667, *Paradise Lost* ranks among the greatest of English literature's epic poems. It's a sublime retelling of Adam and Eve's fall from grace and expulsion from Eden. Notes by John A. Himes. 480pp. 5³⁄₁₆ x 8¼. 0-486-44287-X

PASSING, Nella Larsen. Married to a successful physician and prominently ensconced in society, Irene Redfield leads a charmed existence — until a chance encounter with a childhood friend who has been "passing for white." 112pp. 5⅜ x 8½. 0-486-43713-2

PERSPECTIVE DRAWING FOR BEGINNERS, Len A. Doust. Doust carefully explains the roles of lines, boxes, and circles, and shows how visualizing shapes and forms can be used in accurate depictions of perspective. One of the most concise introductions available. 33 illustrations. 64pp. 5⅜ x 8½. 0-486-45149-6

PERSPECTIVE MADE EASY, Ernest R. Norling. Perspective is easy; yet, surprisingly few artists know the simple rules that make it so. Remedy that situation with this simple, step-by-step book, the first devoted entirely to the topic. 256 illustrations. 224pp. 5⅜ x 8½. 0-486-40473-0

THE PICTURE OF DORIAN GRAY, Oscar Wilde. Celebrated novel involves a handsome young Londoner who sinks into a life of depravity. His body retains perfect youth and vigor while his recent portrait reflects the ravages of his crime and sensuality. 176pp. 5³⁄₁₆ x 8¼. 0-486-27807-7

PRIDE AND PREJUDICE, Jane Austen. One of the most universally loved and admired English novels, an effervescent tale of rural romance transformed by Jane Austen's art into a witty, shrewdly observed satire of English country life. 272pp. 5³⁄₁₆ x 8¼. 0-486-28473-5

THE PRINCE, Niccolò Machiavelli. Classic, Renaissance-era guide to acquiring and maintaining political power. Today, nearly 500 years after it was written, this calculating prescription for autocratic rule continues to be much read and studied. 80pp. 5³⁄₁₆ x 8¼. 0-486-27274-5

QUICK SKETCHING, Carl Cheek. A perfect introduction to the technique of "quick sketching." Drawing upon an artist's immediate emotional responses, this is an extremely effective means of capturing the essential form and features of a subject. More than 100 black-and-white illustrations throughout. 48pp. 11 x 8¼. 0-486-46608-6

RANCH LIFE AND THE HUNTING TRAIL, Theodore Roosevelt. Illustrated by Frederic Remington. Beautifully illustrated by Remington, Roosevelt's celebration of the Old West recounts his adventures in the Dakota Badlands of the 1880s, from round-ups to Indian encounters to hunting bighorn sheep. 208pp. 6¼ x 9¼. 0-486-47340-6

THE RED BADGE OF COURAGE, Stephen Crane. Amid the nightmarish chaos of a Civil War battle, a young soldier discovers courage, humility, and, perhaps, wisdom. Uncanny re-creation of actual combat. Enduring landmark of American fiction. 112pp. 5³⁄₁₆ x 8¼. 0-486-26465-3

RELATIVITY SIMPLY EXPLAINED, Martin Gardner. One of the subject's clearest, most entertaining introductions offers lucid explanations of special and general theories of relativity, gravity, and spacetime, models of the universe, and more. 100 illustrations. 224pp. 5⅜ x 8½. 0-486-29315-7

REMBRANDT DRAWINGS: 116 Masterpieces in Original Color, Rembrandt van Rijn. This deluxe hardcover edition features drawings from throughout the Dutch master's prolific career. Informative captions accompany these beautifully reproduced landscapes, biblical vignettes, figure studies, animal sketches, and portraits. 128pp. 8⅜ x 11. 0-486-46149-1

THE ROAD NOT TAKEN AND OTHER POEMS, Robert Frost. A treasury of Frost's most expressive verse. In addition to the title poem: "An Old Man's Winter Night," "In the Home Stretch," "Meeting and Passing," "Putting in the Seed," many more. All complete and unabridged. 64pp. 5³⁄₁₆ x 8¼. 0-486-27550-7

ROMEO AND JULIET, William Shakespeare. Tragic tale of star-crossed lovers, feuding families and timeless passion contains some of Shakespeare's most beautiful and lyrical love poetry. Complete, unabridged text with explanatory footnotes. 96pp. 5³⁄₁₆ x 8¼. 0-486-27557-4

SANDITON AND THE WATSONS: Austen's Unfinished Novels, Jane Austen. Two tantalizing incomplete stories revisit Austen's customary milieu of courtship and venture into new territory, amid guests at a seaside resort. Both are worth reading for pleasure and study. 112pp. 5⅜ x 8½. 0-486-45793-1

THE SCARLET LETTER, Nathaniel Hawthorne. With stark power and emotional depth, Hawthorne's masterpiece explores sin, guilt, and redemption in a story of adultery in the early days of the Massachusetts Colony. 192pp. 5³⁄₁₆ x 8¼. 0-486-28048-9

THE SEASONS OF AMERICA PAST, Eric Sloane. Seventy-five illustrations depict cider mills and presses, sleds, pumps, stump-pulling equipment, plows, and other elements of America's rural heritage. A section of old recipes and household hints adds additional color. 160pp. 8⅜ x 11. 0-486-44220-9

SELECTED CANTERBURY TALES, Geoffrey Chaucer. Delightful collection includes the General Prologue plus three of the most popular tales: "The Knight's Tale," "The Miller's Prologue and Tale," and "The Wife of Bath's Prologue and Tale." In modern English. 144pp. 5³⁄₁₆ x 8¼. 0-486-28241-4

SELECTED POEMS, Emily Dickinson. Over 100 best-known, best-loved poems by one of America's foremost poets, reprinted from authoritative early editions. No comparable edition at this price. Index of first lines. 64pp. 5³⁄₁₆ x 8¼. 0-486-26466-1

SIDDHARTHA, Hermann Hesse. Classic novel that has inspired generations of seekers. Blending Eastern mysticism and psychoanalysis, Hesse presents a strikingly original view of man and culture and the arduous process of self-discovery, reconciliation, harmony, and peace. 112pp. 5³⁄₁₆ x 8¼. 0-486-40653-9

SKETCHING OUTDOORS, Leonard Richmond. This guide offers beginners step-by-step demonstrations of how to depict clouds, trees, buildings, and other outdoor sights. Explanations of a variety of techniques include shading and constructional drawing. 48pp. 11 x 8¼. 0-486-46922-0

Browse over 9,000 books at www.doverpublications.com

SMALL HOUSES OF THE FORTIES: With Illustrations and Floor Plans, Harold E. Group. 56 floor plans and elevations of houses that originally cost less than $15,000 to build. Recommended by financial institutions of the era, they range from Colonials to Cape Cods. 144pp. 8⅜ x 11. 0-486-45598-X

SOME CHINESE GHOSTS, Lafcadio Hearn. Rooted in ancient Chinese legends, these richly atmospheric supernatural tales are recounted by an expert in Oriental lore. Their originality, power, and literary charm will captivate readers of all ages. 96pp. 5⅜ x 8½. 0-486-46306-0

SONGS FOR THE OPEN ROAD: Poems of Travel and Adventure, Edited by The American Poetry & Literacy Project. More than 80 poems by 50 American and British masters celebrate real and metaphorical journeys. Poems by Whitman, Byron, Millay, Sandburg, Langston Hughes, Emily Dickinson, Robert Frost, Shelley, Tennyson, Yeats, many others. Note. 80pp. 5³⁄₁₆ x 8¼. 0-486-40646-6

SPOON RIVER ANTHOLOGY, Edgar Lee Masters. An American poetry classic, in which former citizens of a mythical midwestern town speak touchingly from the grave of the thwarted hopes and dreams of their lives. 144pp. 5³⁄₁₆ x 8¼. 0-486-27275-3

STAR LORE: Myths, Legends, and Facts, William Tyler Olcott. Captivating retellings of the origins and histories of ancient star groups include Pegasus, Ursa Major, Pleiades, signs of the zodiac, and other constellations. "Classic." — *Sky & Telescope.* 58 illustrations. 544pp. 5⅜ x 8½. 0-486-43581-4

THE STRANGE CASE OF DR. JEKYLL AND MR. HYDE, Robert Louis Stevenson. This intriguing novel, both fantasy thriller and moral allegory, depicts the struggle of two opposing personalities — one essentially good, the other evil — for the soul of one man. 64pp. 5³⁄₁₆ x 8¼. 0-486-26688-5

SURVIVAL HANDBOOK: The Official U.S. Army Guide, Department of the Army. This special edition of the Army field manual is geared toward civilians. An essential companion for campers and all lovers of the outdoors, it constitutes the most authoritative wilderness guide. 288pp. 5³⁄₁₆ x 8¼. 0-486-46184-X

A TALE OF TWO CITIES, Charles Dickens. Against the backdrop of the French Revolution, Dickens unfolds his masterpiece of drama, adventure, and romance about a man falsely accused of treason. Excitement and derring-do in the shadow of the guillotine. 304pp. 5³⁄₁₆ x 8¼. 0-486-40651-2

TEN PLAYS, Anton Chekhov. *The Sea Gull, Uncle Vanya, The Three Sisters, The Cherry Orchard,* and *Ivanov,* plus 5 one-act comedies: *The Anniversary, An Unwilling Martyr, The Wedding, The Bear,* and *The Proposal.* 336pp. 5³⁄₁₆ x 8¼. 0-486-46560-8

THE FLYING INN, G. K. Chesterton. Hilarious romp in which pub owner Humphrey Hump and friend take to the road in a donkey cart filled with rum and cheese, inveighing against Prohibition and other "oppressive forms of modernity." 320pp. 5⅜ x 8½. 0-486-41910-X

THIRTY YEARS THAT SHOOK PHYSICS: The Story of Quantum Theory, George Gamow. Lucid, accessible introduction to the influential theory of energy and matter features careful explanations of Dirac's anti-particles, Bohr's model of the atom, and much more. Numerous drawings. 1966 edition. 240pp. 5⅜ x 8½. 0-486-24895-X

TREASURE ISLAND, Robert Louis Stevenson. Classic adventure story of a perilous sea journey, a mutiny led by the infamous Long John Silver, and a lethal scramble for buried treasure — seen through the eyes of cabin boy Jim Hawkins. 160pp. 5³⁄₁₆ x 8¼. 0-486-27559-0

Browse over 9,000 books at www.doverpublications.com

THE TRIAL, Franz Kafka. Translated by David Wyllie. From its gripping first sentence onward, this novel exemplifies the term "Kafkaesque." Its darkly humorous narrative recounts a bank clerk's entrapment in a bureaucratic maze, based on an undisclosed charge. 176pp. 5³⁄₁₆ x 8¼.   0-486-47061-X

THE TURN OF THE SCREW, Henry James. Gripping ghost story by great novelist depicts the sinister transformation of 2 innocent children into flagrant liars and hypocrites. An elegantly told tale of unspoken horror and psychological terror. 96pp. 5³⁄₁₆ x 8¼.   0-486-26684-2

UP FROM SLAVERY, Booker T. Washington. Washington (1856-1915) rose to become the most influential spokesman for African-Americans of his day. In this eloquently written book, he describes events in a remarkable life that began in bondage and culminated in worldwide recognition. 160pp. 5³⁄₁₆ x 8¼.   0-486-28738-6

VICTORIAN HOUSE DESIGNS IN AUTHENTIC FULL COLOR: 75 Plates from the "Scientific American – Architects and Builders Edition," 1885-1894, Edited by Blanche Cirker. Exquisitely detailed, exceptionally handsome designs for an enormous variety of attractive city dwellings, spacious suburban and country homes, charming "cottages" and other structures — all accompanied by perspective views and floor plans. 80pp. 9¼ x 12¼.   0-486-29438-2

VILLETTE, Charlotte Brontë. Acclaimed by Virginia Woolf as "Brontë's finest novel," this moving psychological study features a remarkably modern heroine who abandons her native England for a new life as a schoolteacher in Belgium. 480pp. 5³⁄₁₆ x 8¼.   0-486-45557-2

THE VOYAGE OUT, Virginia Woolf. A moving depiction of the thrills and confusion of youth, Woolf's acclaimed first novel traces a shipboard journey to South America for a captivating exploration of a woman's growing self-awareness. 288pp. 5³⁄₁₆ x 8¼.   0-486-45005-8

WALDEN; OR, LIFE IN THE WOODS, Henry David Thoreau. Accounts of Thoreau's daily life on the shores of Walden Pond outside Concord, Massachusetts, are interwoven with musings on the virtues of self-reliance and individual freedom, on society, government, and other topics. 224pp. 5³⁄₁₆ x 8¼.   0-486-28495-6

WILD PILGRIMAGE: A Novel in Woodcuts, Lynd Ward. Through startling engravings shaded in black and red, Ward wordlessly tells the story of a man trapped in an industrial world, struggling between the grim reality around him and the fantasies his imagination creates. 112pp. 6⅛ x 9¼.   0-486-46583-7

WILLY POGÁNY REDISCOVERED, Willy Pogány. Selected and Edited by Jeff A. Menges. More than 100 color and black-and-white Art Nouveau–style illustrations from fairy tales and adventure stories include scenes from Wagner's "Ring" cycle, *The Rime of the Ancient Mariner, Gulliver's Travels,* and *Faust.* 144pp. 8⅜ x 11.
                                                              0-486-47046-6

WOOLLY THOUGHTS: Unlock Your Creative Genius with Modular Knitting, Pat Ashforth and Steve Plummer. Here's the revolutionary way to knit — easy, fun, and foolproof! Beginners and experienced knitters need only master a single stitch to create their own designs with patchwork squares. More than 100 illustrations. 128pp. 6½ x 9¼.   0-486-46084-3

WUTHERING HEIGHTS, Emily Brontë. Somber tale of consuming passions and vengeance — played out amid the lonely English moors — recounts the turbulent and tempestuous love story of Cathy and Heathcliff. Poignant and compelling. 256pp. 5³⁄₁₆ x 8¼.   0-486-29256-8